Author

Marcel Martinkovič

SPECTRUM SLOVAKIA Series
Volume 35

Coalition Governments and Development of the Party System in Slovakia

PETER LANG   VEDA

Bibliographic Information published by the Deutsche Nationalbibliothek
The Deutsche Nationalbibliothek lists this publication in the Deutsche Nationalbibliografie; detailed bibliographic data is available in the internet at http://dnb.d-nb.de.

Reviewers: Prof. Uroš Pinterič, PhD.
                                              Doc. Yevheniy Haydanka, PhD.

University of Trnava Faculty of Philosophy and Arts Slovak Republic

ISSN 2195-1845
ISBN 978-3-631–83142-7   ISBN 978-80-224-1772-3
Ebook 978-3-631-84998-9
ePub 978-3-631-84999-6
MOBI 978-3-631-85000-8
doi.org/10.3726/b18170

© Peter Lang GmbH   © VEDA, Publishing House
International Academic Publishers   of the Slovak Academy of Sciences
Berlin 2021   Bratislava 2021

www.peterlang.com   www.veda.sav.sk

This publication is part of the output for the VEGA grant. Project No. 1/0131/18 entitled Europe in Movement. Multicausality of Present Democracy Crisis and the Rise of Extremism in Europe and Grant of the University of Trnava no. 4/TU/2018.

Contents

Parliamentary Elections in Slovakia
(1990 – 2016)

Some Remarks on the Importance of Research into Electoral and Party Systems

The aim of this study is to analyze the development of the party system in Slovakia from the establishment of the independent Slovak Republic to the regular parliamentary elections on March 5, 2016. The reason for limiting this research to the above time segment is the fact that our goal was to provide an analysis of the party system in Slovakia and its development with the use of data on political programs of the respective parties, which were published within the framework of the RILE index (Right–left position), an international database of the right-to-left leaning of political parties.[1] This information, which will be used to define the orientation of the programs and leanings of the political parties to the right or to the left in the Slovak party system, can be found in the database published by Social Science Research Center Berlin.[2] The analysis of the theses verbalized in the programmatic documents of the political parties ranges from the first free elections after the change of the regime in the former Czechoslovakia (Slovak National Council-SNR) in 1990 to the parliamentary elections in 2016. Our research focus is mainly on the positional and programmatic development of the parties in the right-left political continuum, characterization of the developmental stages of the party system, and analysis of the programmatic homogeneity or heterogeneity of the coalition governments. We will use the following hypothesis in our study: Reduction of programmatic (ideological) differences of the parliamentary parties (on the RILE scale) and their positioning in the center of the political spectrum creates space for antipolitical, antiestablishment, and antisystemic or radical parties in the party system.

The present publication aims to characterize the basic attributes of the relationship between the electoral and party system and its development. This area of political science is of critical importance to assess the trends in the development of political parties and party systems in the individual countries. A comprehensive evaluation of the development of the party system requires several other factors to be considered that limit the creation of political representation in the individual political systems. When defining these, the political research has been mainly focused on the impact of electoral laws on the creation of political representation.

---

1 RILE index of the manifesto dataset is the estimate of parties' left–right positions.
2 Wissenschaftszentrum Berlin für Sozialforschung (WZB), Social Science Research Center, Berlin – provides the data within the Comparative Manifestos Project (CMP) [on line April 26, 2019]. Available on https://visuals.manifesto-project.wzb.eu/mpdb-shiny/cmp_dashboard_dataset/.

The important works in this area mainly include the works of G. Almond, M. Duverger, J. Blondel, G. Sartori, R. Dahl, S. Rokkan, R. Rose, R. Taageper, A. Lijphart, R. Katz, D. Rae, P. Mair, and others. In our research, we will apply the criteria used by Giovanni Sartori in his works Parties and Party Systems [3] and Comparative Constitutional Engineering. An Inquiry into Structures, Incentives and Outcomes[4]. When defining the attributes that limit the development of the party system, Sartori particularly highlights the structured nature of the party system, voter distribution, and ideological polarization between the relevant parties. The relevance of the parties is characterized by their coalition or blackmailing potential. When categorizing a particular party system according to Sartori's typology, even the other said criteria should be taken into account in addition to the abundance of relevant parties. Other important elements that can affect the overall nature of the party system and its proportionality in the proportional representation systems include the number and size of electoral districts, the threshold value or quorum, list of candidates (fixed, bound, and free), and also the use of electoral quotas (Hare, Droop quota, Hagenbach-Bischoff method, Hare-Niemeyer method, etc.) or divisor (D'Hondt, Sainte-Lagüe, Imperiali, etc.). Due to the nature of the electoral system in Slovakia, which is characterized by a low threshold for entry into the parliament (5% threshold for a political party), and by a single electoral district since 1998, the distorting effect of the method to redistribute the mandates is minimum. On the other hand, the formation of a proportional party system is accompanied by the development toward an unstructured party system. The structural nature of the party system in Slovakia is not final because a large segment of voters make their decisions based on sympathy for the leader and not according to the program priorities of the relevant party or its abstract image (Sartori, 2001: 49). Based on the research into the relationship and impact of electoral laws on the nature of the party system, Sartori has defined four basic laws (Sartori, 2001: 59-60), which specify the variability of relations between the electoral and party system much more accurately than Duverger's rules defining the relation between the election type and the number of parties (Duverger, 2016: 231-280).[5] The third and fourth Sartori's laws relate to the proportional representation systems. The third law refers to

---

3 (Sartori, 2005: 17-466).

4 (Sartori, 2001: 5-238).

5 For more information on Sartori's criticism of Duverger's rules defining the relation between the electoral and party systems, or Arend Liphart's concept of consensual democracy see in: Novák, M. (ed.): Strany, voľby a demokracie. Od Duvergera k Sartorimu a dále. 2016: 15-432).

the situation where there exists a systemic structure in the party system, which has a reductive effect on the number of parties in the Parliament. The reductive effect of the electoral system is also highlighted by its disproportionality. The development of Slovak electoral and party system since 1990 is most precisely characterized by Sartori's fourth law. "In the absence of a systemic structure and an expectation of a clear (or almost clear) proportional representation, that is, equal (relatively equal) input costs for all parties, there can be as many parties as the quota allows" (Sartori, 2001: 60). Based on this statement, we may conclude that in the case of the political system in the Slovak Republic, the national political representation is created by the rules that lead to a sincere election. At the national parliament level, the Slovak electoral system affects the choice of a political party only minimally because the whole country is a single electoral district, and the criteria for limiting the entry into the Parliament are low (electoral deposit and the number of signatures to register a political party – at least 10 000, etc.).[6] Therefore, in the parliamentary elections we do not see strategic choices, as is the case in the two-round majority system (The Fifth French Republic) or in the relative majority voting system (Great Britain). The proportional representation system tends to produce coalition governments, thus exerting a lower pressure on the voter and greater pressure on the political representation. The political skills of the representation determine the potential for a stable and efficient inter-party cooperation at the parliamentary and executive level. This is, however, limited by several factors, ranging from the nature and number of cleavage lines, to voter volatility, and to the functioning of the party structures. Even for this reason, the development of the Slovak party system shows a tendency toward the fragmentation of the party spectrum. This factor, along with the lack of structure in the party system, which often generates parties with outstanding personalities rather than programmatic solutions, low level of civic awareness of the majority population and "systemic polarization" (Sartori, 2001: 56), is the biggest problem of the party system after 30 years of democratic consolidation.

The unfinished consolidation of the party system in the Slovak Republic after 1993 is coupled with fluctuations in voter volatility. Because the above variables determined the formation of political representation and had an impact on the formation of political parties and their activities and cooperation within the government coalitions, we will characterize the

---

6 The conditions for the emergence of political parties and their registration in the Slovak Republic are regulated by Act no. 85/2005 Coll. on political parties and political movements, as amended.

party development using the basic categories of party systems, such as bipartisanship, moderate pluralism, and polarized pluralism. We consider the analysis of the various development stages of a party system to be an important factor that can help us understand the development at the level of executive representation and formation of coalition governments, which are a natural component – and a consequence – of the proportional representation systems.

Our methodological approach to examine the development of the party system includes a combination of descriptive, empirical, and normative approaches. This functional approach (Sartori, 1993, 20) is based on the need for a combination of qualified approaches to the definition of selected political aspects (effects of the electoral system on the voter, polarization of the party system, ideological orientation of the party program, degree of confrontation in political competition, structured nature of the party system, concentration of power around the party leader, centralization of party structures, etc.) and quantification of selected data (citizen participation rate in elections, proportional representation of political parties in the government based on the mandates, operationalization of the political programs, programmatic heterogeneity and homogeneity of the coalitions, etc.). Only a combination of these approaches can make room for a more comprehensive understanding of the political development in Slovakia and its basic attributes.

Our analysis of the development of the Slovak party system only covers the parliamentary political parties.

Introduction

In order to join the National Council of the Slovak Republic, the parties had to exceed the 3% threshold in the first free elections after 1989. With the adoption of Act no. 104/1992 Coll., this parliamentary threshold increased to 5%. The reason was the unification of the electoral threshold throughout the country because this level was also used in the Federal Parliament and the Czech National Council. At the same time, the conditions for the pre-election coalitions were defined in 1992. The coalition the threshold was set to 7% composed of two or three parties. For the coalitions composed of four or more parties, the threshold was set to 10%. This adjustment meant an increase in the reductive effect of the proportional electoral system, which also triggered a slump in valid electoral votes.[7] Since the establishment of the democratic order in 1990, the Slovak political scene is the characteristic of predominant party in the party system. However, only the government of Direction – Social Democracy (SMER-SD) in the years 2012–2016 fully meets the Sartori's criterion for a system with a predominant party, as this party was able to govern without any coalition partners and with the parliamentary majority (Sartori, 2005: 212). In the previous period, this predominant position in the Slovak party system was almost attained by Movement for a Democratic Slovakia (HZDS). This party ruled the country as a separate entity with the support of Slovak National Party (SNS) from June 24, 1992, to October 11, 1992, when SNS officially confirmed its entry into the ruling coalition. Otherwise, HZDS played an important role in the coalition government of Vladimír Mečiar from December 13, 1994, to October 30, 1998, and in the first government of Robert Fico from July 4, 2006, to July 10, 2010. The outlined development of the party system shows a tendency of voters to favor a single party, usually with a strong charismatic or a populist leader whose rhetoric, to a varying degree, advocates the principle of state etatism. From 1992 to 1998, this role in the system of political parties was played by V. Mečiar's HZDS, and People's Party – Movement for a Democratic Slovakia (ĽS-HZDS since 2003). After the parliamentary elections in 1998, HZDS was dislodged by (hitherto dominant body in governments from 1992 to 1998) the opposition project titled Slovak Democratic Coalition (SDK) with Mikuláš Dzurinda as its leader. This project integrated the opposition parties; however, it has never become a long-term and preferred political body due to its transformative decisions in the socio-economic area. De facto, it was not an ideologically unified political party with clear party structures. The relevance of SDK and its participation in Mikuláš Dzurinda's government in the period October 30, 1998–October 16, 2002, was based on the inter-party cooperation between the then opposition parties. A more intensive cooperation started in 1996 by forming the so-called preelection Blue Coalition. The formal integration of the opposition parties during the government of Vladimír Mečiar was com-

---

7 Compared to the parliamentary elections in 1990, in which 256,766 valid votes were lost, the number in the 1992 elections rose to 733,511. The total increase of lost votes as a result of the new electoral rules reached 476,745 in 1992. The largest parties that did not exceed the 5% threshold included the Civic Democratic Party (ODS) (124,503); Democratic Party – Civic Democratic Party (DS-ODS) (102,058); Slovak Christian Democratic Movement (SKDH) (94,162); and the Green Party of Slovakia (SZS) (66,010). Statistical Office of the Slovak Republic [on line April 26, 2019] Available on http://volby.statistics.sk/nrsr/snr1992/volby92s/pph92.htm.

pleted in 1998 under the pressure of ad hoc changes in the electoral law. The importance of integrating the opposition parties was also supported by the coalition potential of the new parties, Party of Civic Understanding (SOP) in 1998 and Alliance of the New Citizen (ANO) in 2002, when the Mečiar's HZDS was still able to win more electoral votes but its coalition potential lowered. This fact was evident in the high number of electoral votes for HZDS in the 1992, 1994, 1998, and 2002 parliamentary elections,[8] but also by a gradual loss of coalition partners to create a majority government. An important change in the party system occurred after the collapse of the antimečiar project with the wide preelection coalition led by SDK. It resulted in the formation of a standalone political party – Slovak Democratic and Christian Union (SDKÚ) – in 2000. This party, after a merger with the Democratic Party (DS) in 2006, formed SDKÚ-DS as a political party. This political body became the most influential party in the right based on the number of electoral votes in the period 2002–2010. However, it never had the level of voter support of the centrist HZDS in the 1990s and on the verge of the millennium. Nevertheless, the coalition potential of SDK (and later SDKÚ) led by Mikuláš Dzurinda was sufficient enough to create a coalition government in 1998–2002 and 2002–2006. The qualitative change toward the consolidation of the Slovak party system took place in the period 2002–2004 on the left side of the spectrum. After the disintegration of the left (in the period 1994–2003), this development stage of the political system was the characteristic of the integration of small left-wing parties into SMER. SMER subsequently replaced HZDS as a party and it could effectively mobilize the largest number of voters. In 2005, it changed its name to Direction – SMER-SD and Robert Fico became its head. SMER-SD won the largest number of votes in the parliamentary elections in 2006 (671,185 votes – 29.14%), 2010 (880,111 votes – 34.79%), 2012 and 2016. In the early elections in 2012, it won 1,134,280 electoral votes, which equates to 44.41% of the total number of voters. Based on such voter support, SMER-SD was able to create a majority government just by itself. It also won the 2016 elections. In the last parliamentary elections, it won 737,481 votes, that is, -28.28%, and defended the position of the strongest coalition party in the minimum winning coalition SMER-SD, SNS, and Most-Híd.

These circumstances are a mirror to the development of the party system in the Slovak Republic, which was mothballed by the amendment of the electoral law for parliamentary elections, which was passed by

---

8 Statistical Office of the Slovak Republic [on line April 26, 2019]. Available on http://volby. statistics.sk/index.html.

Mečiar's government (HZDS, SNS, and Workers' Association of Slovakia (ZRS)) before the 1998 elections. The then government of V. Mečiar (HZDS, SNS, and ZRS)[9] passed an amendment of the electoral law to favor their position against the then opposition parties. This legislative change has established the criteria, which distorted the development of the Slovak party system and negatively limited it to this day. Among others, we can mention the 5% intracoalition clause for all parties in the preelection coalition, and the introduction of a single nation-wide list of candidates per political party. The whole country has become one single electoral district whereas the original parliamentary elections in Slovakia were held in four electoral districts. This major change led to a greater degree of centralization of the parties, which created negative conditions for their regional and local structures. The negative consequences and the oligarchic nature of the parties are still visible in the non-transparent links to the economic interest groups, which started during the period of uncontrolled privatization of state property in the 1990s and at the beginning of the millennium. Such a harsh interference into the electoral law created space for particular parties with a strong or populist charismatic leader at the expense of the formation of an abstract image of ideologically and programmatically profiled parties. Mečiar's modification of the electoral law for the parliamentary elections, whose aim was to marginalize the opposition and their preelection cooperation, negatively affected the development of the party system and the consolidation of political parties in the Slovak Republic. It hindered the creation of a programmatically structured party system, in which the agenda, ideological anchoring, and well-developed organizational structures are key for their consolidation, to the detriment of the parties with notable charismatic personalities (Sartori, 2001: 49–50). Despite the criticism of the opposition leaders – M. Dzurinda, J. Čarnogurský, E. Kukan, J. Langoš, and others – their parties and representatives failed to eliminate the distorting elements in the electoral law when they won the majority vote in the 1998 parliamentary elections. For this reason, the existence of a single electoral district in the parliamentary elections limits the development of the party structures at the local and regional level.[10] Since

---

9 Slovak National Party (SNS), a conservative-nationalist party, which is committed to the ideas of the historic SNS established in the years 1871–1938. Workers' Association of Slovakia - ZRS, an extreme left-wing socialist body that was formed from the post-communist Party of the Democratic Left (SDĽ) on April 26, 1994.

10 This is visible, for example, in the advent of the so-called independent candidates (NEKA) in the Regional Self-Government elections to the (in Slovak) VUCs and local and municipal authorities to the detriment of partisan candidates. In the case of local authorities, the

1998, the parties have not been encouraged to systematically develop their activities at the local level because all they need to function in Parliament is a narrow range of party elites and district or regional structures. This results in a credibility crisis of the parties, which, coupled with increased corruption in public life after 2016, was also manifested by the establishment of a right-wing extremist and latently antisystemic party Kotleba – People's Party Our Slovakia, Kotleba -Ľudová strana naše Slovensko (K-ĽS NS) in the Parliament. The current centralization of partisan politics in Slovakia is paradoxically affected by the fact that a number of parties, which clearly defined themselves against the originally established incumbents, have an even smaller member base and leadership than the original parties (e.g., Freedom and Solidarity – SaS; Ordinary People and Independent Personalities – OĽaNO; Network – Sieť; We Are Family – Boris Kollár – Sme rodina – Boris Kollár; Kotleba – People's Party Our Slovakia, etc.).[11] This would be a natural phenomenon in the newly established parties, but some of the aforementioned parties have been already operating on a parliamentary level for more than one term (the liberal SaS since 2009 and the conservative, antipolitical, and antiestablishment movement OĽaNO since 2011), and yet, they made no significant progress in the development of their regional and local party structures. One of the risks associated with the parties represented on the national level mainly through the work of a single leader and a small group of his/her co-workers is that they quickly turn into oligarchic structures.[12] At the same time, this minimizes the impact of lower and local levels of the party structure on the internal development of democratic environment. The phenomenon of the so-called primaries, or inner referendums on key questions of partisan ori-

NEKA rate has increased since 2001 when regional governments were established in Slovakia from the original 18 candidates (4.48% of the total number of members) to 161 independent candidates in 2017 (i.e., 39.42% of the total number of members). The crisis of credibility of the political parties is also expressed through the continuous growth in the number of independent candidates, and even in the local elections. Since 2002 when NEKA took 13.46% of the parliamentary seats, their proportion rose to 28,91% in the last communal and municipal elections in 2014. For more see: Klus, Martinkovič, 2019: 193–198 and Martinkovič, 2018: 55–60.

11 For the development of the member base of select parties in the period 2006-2017, see on chapter Charts and Tables.

12 This natural tendency in the development of party structures was first characterized by Robert Michels, a representative of classical elitism. After the publication of research on German political parties, he claimed in his work titled Zur Soziologie des Parteiwesens in der modernen Demokratie (1911) that regardless of their ideological orientation and program, the parties tend to become oligarchic. For issues related to the so-called iron law of oligarchy, see, for example, Sartori, 1993: 150-153.

entation and governmental cooperation, etc., is virtually absent in the Slovak party system. This low rate of participation and responsibility of the local and regional structures in the overall activities of the political entities is subsequently reflected in the reduction of functionality of the parties as key elements in an effective functioning of the democratic system. When combined with the reduction of ideological differences between the parties, this may create space for extremists, particularly in non-voters and disgruntled voters of the incumbent parties.

If the established parties are unable to perform the basic functions such as settling the disputes between different social groups, formulating a comprehensive political program, generating a credible political leadership, socializing the citizens, facilitating communication between the citizens and the state, ensuring the organization of government and its control in the context of public interests, the overall functioning of the institution and the legitimacy of representative democracy will diminish. If this function cannot be met by the established parties, it can be assumed by the newly emerging entities, which are trying to win over the established parties and articulate themselves in terms of relations and ideology. This radicalization of political life and objectives is then reflected in their activities and ability to aggregate the portion of public support of those citizens who no longer trust the democratic institutions. The more isolated the parties, the stronger their extremist and populist attitudes. In such an environment, the negative development and isolation of the narrow partisan presidencies in the established and pro-democracy parties is getting even stronger, and allows the parties to connect with coercive interest groups more freely and without substantial control of the member base. The legitimacy of incumbent pro-democracy parties is systematically hampered by the unwillingness of the leaders to bear political responsibility for the alleged corrupt behavior of their representatives. One of the reasons why this situation occurs across all the established political parties in Slovakia (People's Party – Movement for a Democratic Slovakia (ĽS-HZDS), SNS, KDH,[13] SDKÚ-DS, SMER-SD, Most-Híd, SaS, etc.), which had executive responsibility, is the quantitatively narrow leadership of these parties. The second reason is the reluctance of the professionally qualified people to be engaged in partisan politics, fueled by a general distrust toward politics. At the level of national political life, this results in the emergence of crony parties, which give rise to the so-called crony parliamentarism (Klíma, 2015: 206). Apart from numerous instances of corruption, this trend is also

---

13 Christian Democratic Movement (KDH).

characterized by a higher level of instability in the exercise of power. The ensuing instability of the structures of political parties has an effect on the constant partisan divisions and emergence of new bodies and actors that can make it through the elections. For example, the new leftist SOP in 1998; the liberal Alliance of New Citizens (ANO) and the SMER in 2002; the civil-liberal Most-Híd and liberal SaS in 2010; OĽaNO in 2012; and the right-wing extremist K–ĽS NS, the movement We Are Family – Boris Kollár, and the rightist Network in 2016. This negative decomposition of the party system in Slovakia goes hand in hand with the increased partisan unreliability in public opinion polls. The increased polarization of relations between the parties (which not always corresponds with ideological polarization) runs in parallel with such developments not only in Slovakia, but also in the neighboring countries of the Visegrad Group (V4). This development is often accompanied by the rise of antisystemic and antipolitical or antiestablishment parties (Schedler, 2002: 36–50) on the national level and proliferation of alienating political culture (Klicperová-Baker, Feierabend, et al., 2007: 21). A significant impact on the Slovak party system (in the light of party transformation in the Czech Republic) was made by the all-European tendency of the past decade, in particular, right-wing populism, anti-immigrant rhetoric, manipulation with the notion of Euroskepticism (Haydanka, 2018: 189).[14] This fact accounts for the strengthening of the party institute of antisystem parties, accompanied by a noticeable increase in populism in the party rhetoric of the leading political actors.

This publication will also attempt to answer the question to what degree the coalition governments that have emerged since the first free elections in 1990 and formed the governing majority in the SNR and NR SR (after the inception of the independent Slovak Republic) up until the elections in 2016 were programmatically homogeneous or heterogeneous. These conclusions are based on the positional value of the political program of each party on the RILE scale. In the final assessment of the nature of individual coalitions, we will also verify the relevance of the hitherto conclusions published in this area. We will focus on verifying the following hypothesis: Is there a correlation between the increasingly blurred programmatic differences between the parliamentary parties and the rise of extremist and antisystemic parties? Our assumption is that the blurring of ideological differences between the parliamentary parties in Slovakia provides ground for the establishment of antisystemic parties in the outer parts of the political spectrum. The antisystemic nature, extremist tenden-

---

14 In this context, see Haydanka, 2020: 253–265.

cies, and extremist bodies will be evaluated with M. Kubát's typology who followed up on the research of antisystemic opposition by G. Sartori and G. Capoccia. In the analysis, he proposed two basic evaluation criteria: The relational variable, which demonstrates the marginal position or isolation of the party vis-a-vis the position of other parties, and the ideological variable, which is manifested by the (de)legitimization of the democratic establishment and representative democracy. At its core, the antisystemic parties have always promoted the delegitimization of democratic institutions, and fostered antidemocratic values and ideology (Kubát, 2010: 83–85), cf. (Sartori, 2005: 137). In the analysis of the party system and its development, we will also highlight the emergence of antipolitical and antiestablishment parties that accept the framework of democratic political competition but systematically challenge the ability of the established parties to address major social problems.

To describe the development of the Slovak party system, we will use the results from a quantitative analysis of the election programs using the Comparative Manifestos Project (CMP) approach.[15] The reason for this combined quantitative and qualitative research is the fact that the election programs are some of the key objective sources of information about the political orientation of the parties. The information in the programs is an operational rendition of the political aims and objectives of the parties. The results of the analysis are then processed as data, which allows us to determine the approximate position of the program on the RILE scale. We would like to note that this research is not focused on evaluating the specific decisions of the parties and their leaders or coalitions. We are aware that the actual political decisions of the parties in the respective governments are limited by a number of non-quantifiable factors, such as the relations of the coalition parties in the government, foreign policy, or the populist tendencies of their leaders, etc. For this reason, the government measures implemented in practice do not always reflect their political programs. This research is also important in order to unify the research methodology of the party systems and the subsequent relevance in the comparison of the development trends. The use of a quantitative approach to analyze the parties and the party system with the RILE index is not very typical in the Slovak political system.[16] The programmatic aspects

---

15 Wissenschaftszentrum Berlin für Sozialforschung (WZB) provides the data within the CMP. [on line 26.4.2019] Available on https://manifesto-project.wzb.eu.
16 An exception is the work by (Pinterič, Žúborová, 2012: 349-368), which uses different analytical criteria and it differentiates between the political and economic plane in the orientation and positions of the political parties.

attributed to the rightist parties on the RILE scale are the following: positive perception of armed forces, constitutionalism, national interests, traditional morality, respect for freedoms and human rights, emphasis on law and order, development of free business, political authority, market economy, and a parallel emphasis on the limitations of the welfare state and protectionism. The programmatic aspects attributed to the leftist parties include market regulation, controlled economy, decolonization, promotion of peace, democracy, strong influence of the state in the economy, expansion of the welfare state, protection of workers, government involvement in education, internationalism, etc. (Budge, Meyer, 2013: 88). A comprehensive assessment of the parties and the nature of the coalitions should therefore include the concrete decisions, speeches, and rhetoric of each party in addition to the quantifiable RILE data. Given the scope of this work, however, this hardly attainable in the present publication – the same can be said about the analysis of the positives and negatives of the individual methodological approaches to the study of parties and party systems. The present publication has the ambition to contribute to the application of internationally accepted criteria for assessing the political parties on the party system in the Slovak political community.

The determination of ideological positions of the parties will be based on the classic ideological typology of political parties on the RILE axis.[17] To shed some more light on the RILE index, we would like to remind the readers of the fact that this system uses seven evaluation criteria to determine the ideological positioning of the parties. The areas of concern are as follows: foreign relations, freedom and democracy, political system, economy, prosperity and quality of life, social arrangement, and social groups. This type of quantitative analysis is done by encoding/ranking the election programs using the CMP method.[18] This method is aimed at determining the ideological positions of the parties before particular parliamentary elec-

---

An analysis using the RILE index was applied, for example, to the Polish context – see the study by Kinga Wojtas named *Coalition politics in Poland in the years 1991–2015 – in search of rules*, pp 23–45. In: Rudowski, A., Sulkowski, M., et al. (2017): *Poland in the European Union – perspectives of membership*, CSWUP, Warsaw. In this context also see Marchuk, 2008.

17 The most well-known approach to the analysis of the positioning and programming of political parties was presented in the work by Klaus von Beyme who identified the following types of parties/political bodies: 1. liberal and radical parties; 2. conservative parties; 3. socialist and social-democratic parties; 4. christian-democratic parties; 5. communist parties; 6. farmers' parties; 7. regional and ethnic parties; 8. extreme right-wing parties; 9. ecological parties. (Beyme, 1985: 23–24).

18 For more information, see the Coding Scheme. [on line 19.9.2018] Available on http://electoraldemocracy.com/wp-content/uploads/2009/06/Coding-Scheme-08092011.pdf.

tions, and it has more than a political-economic dimension. Despite the fact that several authors note the trend of reducing the ideological distance between the parties and/or emergence of similarities between the relevant parties (Keller, 2001: 121–122), the approach of dividing the parties on the RILE scale is used in most analyses of party systems. This is caused by the fact that the traditional political symbolism and programmatic priorities of the parties in terms of, for example, activities in the economic and social fields helps the citizens to determine the political orientation of the parties in political competition.

The development of the Slovak party system from the beginning of the democratic political order after the revolution in 1989 and 1990 is characteristic by an observable preference for the parties with charismatic and rhetorically gifted leaders and fragmentation of the party system.[19] This is then intensified by the lack of interest of the party elites to create and develop an environment for the ideological intra-party factions. The political tensions within the party elites often result in splitting the party in two. This scenario was observed in HZDS, KDH, SNS, SDĽ, SDKÚ-DS, ANO, SMK, SaS, etc. The ever so frequent divisions of the parties testify to the fact that the party elites in Slovakia are not able to tolerate any differences of opinion or fractions within the already established parties. For this reason, we witnessed the emergence of new parties in the Slovak party system, which even made it into Parliament (e.g., ZRS in 1994; SDK and SOP in 1998; SDKÚ, ANO, and SMER in 2002; SaS and Most-Híd in 2010; OĽaNO in 2012; Network, K-ĽS NS, the movement We Are Family – Boris Kollár in 2016). The fragmentation and fission of political parties, combined with a higher rate of electoral volatility[20] (fluctuation of electoral preferences), causes a relatively high instability in the Slovak political system, which contributes to maintaining the programmatic polarization even in the opposition.

The parties and their programs can also be illustrated in the context of valency (common and overlapping themes and objectives) and positional themes that differentiate the programmatic objectives of the

---

19 The proportionality of the party system in Slovakia is limited to a single electoral district, low threshold for the parties to make it into Parliament, proportional conversion of votes to mandates (the Hagenbach-Bischoff quota), and low voter bail (in 2016 it totaled to 16,596 euro), etc.

20 For more information on volatility, see Gyárfášová, O., Bahna, M., Slosiarik, M., 2017: Sila nestálosti: volatilita voličov na Slovensku vo voľbách 2016. Středoevropské politické studie, Vol. 19, No. 1, pp. 1–24. ISSN 1212-7817 [on line 25.4.2019]. Available on https://journals.muni.cz/cepsr/article/view/6861.

parliamentary parties in the relevant election periods. When analyzing the developmental trends in the party system, we will try to define the types of coalitions and their programmatic heterogeneity or homogeneity. To characterize the coalitions, we will use the RILE index of the said parties, which is going to be used to determine the programmatic differences of the coalition parties. Similarly, the RILE index will be used in the analysis of development of the political system by defining the variable (programmatic) tensions between the positionally extreme parliamentary parties.

Parliamentary Elections in 1990

Our research will start with the first free elections after the change of government in 1989. The elections into the Slovak National Council were held on June 8 and 9, 1990. As these were the first free elections since May 1946 and/or from the political changes initiated by the students and dissidents after November 17, 1989, the turnout was high. Up to 95.39% of the eligible voters participated in the elections. Altogether seven political bodies made it into SNR since the parliamentary threshold or quorum was only 3%.

From this point on, usually 5–6 parties with a coalition or extortion potential have always made it into Parliament. This implies that in the context of G. Sartori's typology, the Slovak party system has evolved as an example of extreme pluralism. This format, especially since 1991 (when the dispute between the members of the VPN Coordination Center and V. Mečiar and his sympathizers culminated in March), is characteristic of polarized pluralism as a type of inter-party competition.[21] This tendency was also evident in the last parliamentary elections in 2016 when the number of parties in Parliament increased to eight, and the opposition parties were

---

21 According to G. Sartori, the typology of the party system is viewed as a theoretical concept, which may have different variations and tolerances in practice while maintaining the logic of inter-party rivalry and competition. Polarized pluralism is defined by Sartori as the presence of an antisystemic party, polarized binary opposition, centrist formations, and ideological distance between the parties. This causes the polarization of the party system, predominance of centrifugal tendencies among the parties, an ideologically structured society, emergence of irresponsible opposition, and the policy of triumphalism based on populism. For more information, see Sartori, 2005: 135–147.

ideologically polarized due to the presence of the latently antisystemic and extremist party K-LSNS.[22]

The following bodies made it into the SNR in 1990: the centrist civic movement Public Against Violence (VPN) with 29.35% (991,285) and 48 seats, Christian Democratic Movement (KDH) with 19.21% (648,782) and 17 seats, nationalist SNS with 13.94% (470,984) and 9 seats, socialist Czechoslovak Communist Party (KSČ) with 13.35% (450,855) and 13 seats, the preelection coalition of the Hungarian minority in Slovakia Coexistence - Hungarian Christian - Democratic Movement (ESWMK) with 8.66% (292 636) and 14 seats, civil conservative DS with 4.4% (148,567) and 7 seats, and the environmentally oriented Green Party with 3.49% (117,871) and 6 seats.[23] The government was formed as a minimum winning coalition with 86 of the available 150 seats in the SNR. It consisted of the representatives of VPN, KDH, and DS, with V. Mečiar as its prime minister. Based on the cooperation with VPN prior to the elections, the government was also supported by the Hungarian minority parties although these parties were not part of the official coalition from the very beginning. They joined it in 1991. The political development among the parties led to the emergence of cleavages such as communism vs. anticommunism, center vs. periphery, and nationalism. The coalition operated in the above composition until the dispute in the leadership of the strongest government party - the civic movement VPN. The VPN board removed V. Mečiar as prime minister on April 23, 1991, and replaced him by Ján Čarnogurský, the head of KDH. He then led a minority cabinet with the support of only 61 MPs. This government, however, was not new. Only the prime minister was replaced in the coalition. The first government of V. Mečiar consisted of 18 VPN nominees (in addition to the prime minister, major government positions, such as the Ministry of Finance, Ministry of Foreign Affairs, Ministry of Justice, were populated by VPN); KDH populated 8 ministries (including the Ministry

---

22 We note that Sartori's typology and its categories are viewed as ideal types with practical variability. In actuality, not all the aspects of a given category, as defined by Sartori, have to be met when placing the parties into the individual categories. Despite some deviations (e.g., the absence of antisystemic parties in all individual development stages of the Slovak party system), we are still able to determine the direction of development into a particular party type. Analytically, we are able to determine the party systems even without quantifying the individual programs on the RILE scale. According to Sartori, it is more important to understand the development context of political competition, the relations between the various actants (coalition and opposition), and the nature of their programs in relation to the liberal-democratic principles that engage in the quantification of data.

23 Statistical Office of the Slovak Republic [on line 25.4.2019]. Available on http://volby.statistics.sk/nrsr/snr1990/volby90_s/pph90.htm.

of the Interior and Ministry of Agriculture) and DS ran three ministries (including the Ministry of Industry and Trade and Ministry of Social Affairs). All parties were adequately and proportionally represented in the government with respect to the number of seats in Parliament. An exception was the representatives of DS, who populated more ministries in the government than their proportional election results (Balík, Havlík, et al. 2011: 212). If we follow up on the data obtained through the CMP method, we see that[24] the first government of Vladimír Mečiar exhibited a relatively wide programmatic span among the government parties (32.05) based on the ideological positioning of the parties in the coalition. Nevertheless, some authors dub it the "least winning" and ideologically linked and/or homogeneous coalition (Balík, Havlík, et al. 2011: 196). The reason for such a statement at this development stage of the party system could be the communism vs. anticommunism cleavage, which in a way connected the programs of all ruling parties in order to implement some fundamental political and economic reforms.

We assumed that the parties such as the Czechoslovak Communist Party – KSČ with 13.35% of the votes[25] (RILE index of -16,35) would occupy the left side of the spectrum. However, since the Green Party in Slovakia – SZS (with an index of -17.65) made it into Parliament, the KSČ did not occupy the far-left slot in the Parliament after the first free elections.[26] However, the opposition was ideologically polarized, as it was formed by the radical socialist KSČ and the nationalist SNS, and the coalition of ethnic Hungarians living in Slovakia Coexistence – Hungarian Christian – Democratic Movement (ESWMK). It visibly exhibited the nationalist and socioeconomic cleavage.

The DS had an interesting position in the first government. Despite its declared position as a rightist conservative party, it exhibited leftist traits on the RILE scale (-12.30). The DS occupied the leftmost position within the framework of the ruling coalition (Public against Violence – VPN, KDH, and DS). According to the RILE index, the position of KDH was in line with

---

24 The programmatic characteristics according to the RILE index are calculated by taking the difference between the rightist and leftist topics in the programs. Based on this, the positioning of a particular party is determined on the left-to-right ideological scale.

25 Statistical Office of the Slovak Republic [on line 25.4.2019] Available on http://volby. statistics.sk/nrsr/snr1990/volby90_s/php90.htm.

26 Another reason was the gradual breaking off of relations between the Slovak and Czech communist elites in KSČ, with the reformist socialist wing slowly gaining traction in Slovakia. This later transformed a substantial part of the communist structures into the reformist left-wing social-democratic Party of the Democratic Left (SDĽ). For more information, see Kopeček, 2007: 182–188).

its self-definition as a rightist Christian, conservative party. Similarly, the RILE value of -7.03 applied to VPN due to its multi-disciplinary political nature as a civil and centrist movement, and not a standard ideologically clear party.

Table RILE index of the parliamentary parties in the 1990 elections

SNS	39.22
KDH	19.75
ESWMK	5.26
VPN	-7.03
DS	-12.30
KSČ	-16.35
SZS	-17.65
Variable range of the parliamentary parties and their programs	56.87
Turnout	95.39%
Programmatic differences of the VPN, KDH, and DS coalition	32.05

Source: Manifesto Project. Social Science Research Center Berlin [on line 25.4.2019]. Available on https://visuals.manifesto-project.wzb.eu/mpdb-shiny/cmp_dashboard_dataset/

Chart: Ideological positioning of the parties in 1990 according to the RILE index

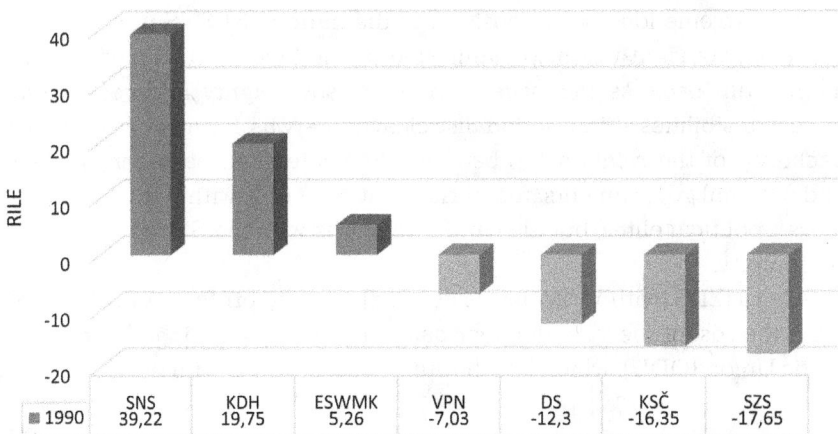

	SNS	KDH	ESWMK	VPN	DS	KSČ	SZS
■ 1990	39,22	19,75	5,26	-7,03	-12,3	-16,35	-17,65

The political program of the minimum winning and ideologically connected coalition VPN, KDH, and DS (100 to -100 on the program evaluation scale) ranked at 32.05 on the RILE scale. Within the context of the ruling parties, only KDH manifested consistency between the program of the party and its general public image and the rhetoric about its ideological orientation as a rightist, Christian-democratic party.

Among the opposition parties, the RILE index showed the relevance of characterizing KSČ as a leftist, socialist body, which was similar to the leftist orientation of SZS and the nationalist-conservative SNS. Conversely, the RILE index showed a noticeable departure from the declared political and ideological orientation of the ruling DS.

After the first free elections in 1990, extreme pluralism began to shape in the Slovak party system (Seven relevant parties made it into Parliament) and polarized pluralism also made its way into the ideological polarization of the opposition parties. The opposition party SNS on the right and SZS on the left side of the spectrum represented the outer extremes of the parliamentary continuum.

After the culmination of a policy dispute between the VPN Coordination Center and V. Mečiar, as its most popular politician, a non-standard conflict line formed in the Slovak political system. This line divided the supporters and opponents of V. Mečiar and gave way to the emergence of the so-called mečiarism vs. antimečiarism (cleavage political liberalism vs. authoritarianism).[27] The preelection coalition of the ethnic parties of the Hungarian minority ESWMK took a centrist stance at 5.26 in the RILE index.

The extreme ideological position of the nationalist SNS in the context of the Slovak right was also manifested by the fact that this party gained momentum because the issue of national sovereignty and reallocation of responsibilities – the nationalist cleavage – was foregrounded on the backdrop of the relationship between the center and periphery (federal and national governments and parliaments) not only within the Czech and Slovak political elites, but also in the relations with the Slovak-Hungarian community.

After HZDS (with V. Mečiar as its head) chipped off from VPN (June 22, 1991), the rest of the VPN member base transformed in to the Civic Democratic Union (ODÚ), which lost the June 1992 elections with only 4.04%.

---

27 For more see Gyárfášová, O. (2018): Strany a voliči na ľavo-pravom kontinuu: konvergencia alebo divergencia? In: Krivý, V. (ed.): Slovenské voľby 2016 retrospektívne analýzy. Bratislava: Sociologický ústav SAV, p. 246.

Parliamentary Elections in 1992

The turnout in the parliamentary elections, which were held on June 5 and 6, 1992, was 84.20% of the eligible voters. Despite the high turnout, it dropped by 11.19% in comparison with the 1990 elections. The number of the parties in SNR was also affected by the new electoral law, which raised the parliamentary threshold to 5%.

In June 1992, the following parties made it into SNR: the centrist movement HZDS with 37.26% (1,148,625 votes) and 74 seats, the ex-communist reformist wing of the KSS Party of the Democratic Left (SDĽ) with 14.70% (453,203 votes) and 29 seats, KDH with 8.89% (273,945 votes) and seats 18, the nationalist SNS with 7.93% (244,527 votes) and 15 seats, and the coalition of the Hungarian minority KDH Együttélés – Spolužitie – Wspólnota – Soužití (MKM – EGY) with 7.42% (228,885 votes) and 14 seats. The Slovak Communist Party, an extreme left party of the non-reformist communists (with 0.76%, i.e., 23,349 votes) did not make it into Parliament. This party was a follower of the original Communist Party of Czechoslovakia and Communist Party of Slovakia (KSS). The extremist rightist Slovak People's Party – SĽS, which built on the authoritarian regime of the fascist Slovak State and the "people's" political tradition (with 0.30%, i.e., 9,129 votes) did not make it into Parliament either.[28]

Due to the disintegration of the broad civil movement VPN which, in addition to the original liberal opposition elites, it also integrated representatives of the dissent and environmental associations, also some of the original communist elites (M. Čalfa, M. Čič, M. Kováč, A. Dubček, and others), the divisions in the party system continued. After the establishment of HZDS, which emerged from VPN, the varying degrees of involvement and continuity of the communist elites continued not only in the above parties, but also in SDĽ, SNS, and other parties (Kopeček, 2006: 160). After the formation of the mečiarism vs. antimečiarism cleavage, the very leader of HZDS Vladimír Mečiar attempted to form the government. His HZDS tried to present itself as a centrist, catch-all party, and declared that it integrated the Christian, national, and social streams. Nevertheless, the confrontational policies of V. Mečiar and his HZDS were the reason for the increasing polarization of parliamentary parties. In the resulting political situation, a wide governmental cooperation of the other parliamentary

---

28 Statistical Office of the Slovak Republic [on line 25.4.2019] Available on http://volby.statistics.sk/nrsr/snr1992/volby92s/php92.htm.

parties, in particular with regard to the rising nationalist cleavage, was un-real. A minority cabinet was formed for the first time in the Slovak political system – supported by the 74 members of Parliament from HZDS. The government thus consisted of the HZDS nominees. Mečiar's minority government had supporters in the nationalist SNS because Ľudovít Černák, its member and chairman (since October 1992), became Minister of Economy. The supporting parties, which had allowed the government to be formed and its mission statement approved, also included the nationalist SNS and the post-communist SDĽ, which supported the non-partisan Jozef Tuchyňa in Mečiar's government. Therefore, due to the presence of the SNS nominee, Mečiar controlled the coalition majority although SNS turned down the offer to officially enter the government. In negotiations with the Czech government headed by the chairman of the Civic Democratic Party (ODS) V. Klaus, this government eventually approved the split and demise of the Czech and Slovak Federal Republic on December 31, 1992. After the establishment of the independent Slovak Republic, the government continued in its original composition and form. The next change occurred on November 10, 1993, when SNS became an official coalition partner of HZDS. This only happened after several members left HZDS and HZDS losing some of the 74 seats in the 150-seat Parliament.[29] From this point on, the official entry of SNS into the coalition was a token of support of the minimum winning and ideologically connected coalition, which had 81 seats in the Parliament. After yet another dispute within HZDS, more MPs left the HZDS parliamentary group, and V. Mečiar's government yet again lost the majority vote in the Parliament.[30]

In this period, we also witnessed a clash between the leader of HZDS Vladimir Mečiar and Michal Kováč, the president of Slovakia and a HZDS nominee. After the loss of ruling majority, the president called on HZDS as a winning party in the elections to appoint a leader with the aim to create a new government. The HZDS representation did not act upon this call. After consultations with other parties, the president nominated Jozef

---

29 Controversy over the style of governance and political objectives broke out between the then prime minister and chairman of HZDS V. Mečiar and his Foreign Minister M. Kňažko (vice-chairman of HZDS) led to a departure Milan Kňažko from HZDS. He established new parliamentary group called Alliance of Democrats of the Slovak Republic (ADS).

30 A similar dispute over the style of governance and political objectives broke out between the then prime minister and chairman of HZDS and his Foreign Minister J. Moravčík. He, along with then deputy prime minister of the Slovak Republic for HZDS Roman Kováč, quit his membership in HZDS and established his own parliamentary group called Alternative to Political Realism (APR). Both groups of MPs who left HZDS in the years 1993 and 1994 (ADS and APR) had created the new Democratic Union of Slovakia (DÚ) in April 1994.

Moravčík as prime minister, who had worked in HZDS before and was the successor to Milan Kňažko as Minister of Foreign Affairs in the same parliamentary term. Moravčík's government (March 15, 1994–December 13, 1994) was composed of KDH, SDĽ, and the former members of HZDS around M. Kňažko (ADS), Jozef Moravčík (APR), and Ľudovít Černák who left SNS. These parties and their leaders formed the Democratic Union of Slovakia (DÚ) in the upcoming early elections in 1994. However, Moravčík's government did not win a majority vote in the National Council (it was only supported by 71 MPs), and his formation had to be supported by the representatives of the Hungarian parliamentary bodies.

When analyzing V. Mečiar's second government, the data obtained by the CMP method indicate that it exhibits very low programmatic differences among the government parties. The programmatic differences in the minimum winning and ideologically connected coalition of the nationally oriented HZDS and SNS reached a level of 1.06 in the RILE index. Both coalition parties maintained a slight preponderance of right-wing topics and were moving around the ideological center. The proportionality between HZDS and SNS in terms of the percentage of mandates and ministerial posts in the government was maintained. Each government party gained a fair share of government power, which was proportionate to the number of its MPs.

The reason for the very low programmatic differences between HZDS and SNS is the SNS and its shift from the extreme right in 1990 with a value of 39.22 to a centrist position with a score of 3.50 in the RILE index. What is interesting is also the score of the charismatic-crony HZDS[31] which, when viewed in the context of chipping off from VPN, moved to the right with a score of 2.44. The original VPN had a RILE score of -7.03 in 1990, which corresponds to a slightly leftist-centrist party. The declared ideological position of HZDS as a universal party and/or catch-all party thus corresponded to its program on the RILE scale. Similarly, KDH remained in the declared position of a rightist Christian-democratic party. From the original value of 19.75 in 1990, KDH moved to the right to 26.34 on the RILE scale in 1992 and became the outermost party on the right. SDĽ as a transformed post-communist, social democratic party, moved to the center right of the political continuum. All programs of the parliamentary parties showed the values of rightist parties and most of them were centrist, with values around zero. An exception was the Christian-conservative KDH, which took the position of a rightist conservative prosystem party.

---

31 For more information on charismatic-crony party, see Kopeček, 2006: 268–274.

If we were to characterize J. Moravčík's government, which consisted of KDH, SDĽ, and the MPs who left HZDS and SNS (ADS, APR), it would have exhibited far greater programmatic differences than the second Mečiar's cabinet, as its programmatic differences spanned from the clear-cut right-wing KDH (26,34) to the extremely leftist SDĽ (1.41). The overall programmatic differences of Moravčík's ideologically heterogeneous coalition government scored 24.93 on the RILE scale. In Moravčík's government, SDĽ was underrepresented in terms of the number of mandates in the Parliament and government (40.8% and 33%) and the MPs who left HZDS and SNS and congealed through ADS and APR into the civic-liberal DÚ before the elections were overrepresented (33.8% and 40%) (Balík, Havlík, et al., 2011: 212).

Most of the relevant parties in the party system, however, had a rightist-centrist character on the RILE scale. This aspect was also reflected in the lower ideological distance between the parties, and the variable tensions in the party system lowered from 56.87 in 1990 to 24.93 points on the RILE scale. This effect was manifested in the creation of an ideologically homogeneous government majority of HZDS and SNS after the 1992 elections. This later cooperated as SNS as a supporting party of the official HZDS minority government of V. Mečiar, and since November 11, 1993, in the form of an official minimum winning ruling coalition of HZDS and SNS, which ended up by the disintegration of the (mainly) HZDS parliamentary group.

Table RILE index of the parliamentary parties in the 1992 elections

KDH	26.34
ADS	11.86
SNS	3.50
MKM – EGY	5.26
HZDS	2.44
SDĽ	1.41
Variable range of the parliamentary parties and their programs	24.93
Turnout	84.20%
Programmatic differences of the HZDS, SNS coalition	1.06
Programmatic differences of the KDH, SDĽ, ADS coalition, and KMK-EGY as a supporting party	24.93

Source: Manifesto Project. Social Science Research Center Berlin [on line 25.4.2019]. Available on https://visuals.manifesto-project.wzb.eu/mpdb-shiny/cmp_dashboard_dataset/

Chart: Ideological positioning of the parties in 1992 according to the RILE index

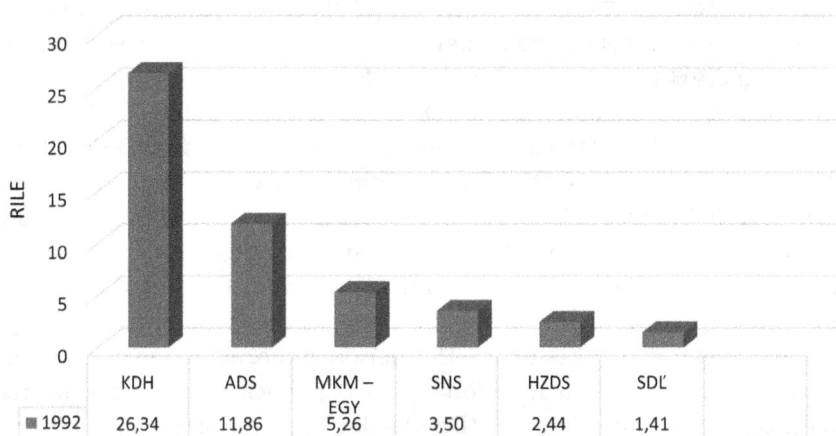

	KDH	ADS	MKM – EGY	SNS	HZDS	SDĽ
■ 1992	26,34	11,86	5,26	3,50	2,44	1,41

Despite the lower variable range of the parliamentary parties, the party system maintained a trajectory toward the stabilization of extreme and polarized pluralism. We witnessed the emergence of cleavages such as urban-rural, ethnic-nationalist, and mainly the atypical cleavage mečiarism vs. antimečiarism (Madleňák, 2012: 31–37), which distorted the development of the Slovak party system for the next 16 years until the 2010 election. In the 2010 elections, HZDS did not exceed the election threshold for entry to the Slovak Parliament, which initiated its political marginalization and gradual demise. Despite the polarizing political situation, however, no extremist and antisystemic parties made it into Parliament at this development stage of the Slovak party system.

Early Parliamentary Elections in 1994

The early elections were held on September 30–October 1, 1994, with a participation of 75.65% of the eligible voters. The reason for the early elections was the social democratic party SDĽ and its head Peter Weiss who thought that this move would bring the party an indisputable legitimacy and higher representation in the government. These elections were the first early elections held in the newly established Slovak Republic.

In 1994, the parliamentary elections were won by the centrist movement HZDS-RSS with 34.97% (1,005,488 votes) and 61 seats, socialist-oriented ZRS, with 7.35% (211,321 votes) and 13 mandates and the conservative-nationalist SNS with 5.40% (155,359 votes) and 9 seats.[32] The preelection social-democratic coalition Common Choice (SDĽ together with the SZS and Farmers' Movement HP SR and the Social Democratic Party of Slovakia (SDSS) had 10.42% (299,496) and 8 seats.[33] The Parliament was also populated by the KDH with 10.08% (289,987 votes) and 17 seats, the new liberal party DÚ with 8.57% (246,444 votes) that is, 15 mandates, and the ethnic electoral Hungarian Coalition (MKDH, ESWS, and MOS) – MK with 10.19% (292,936) votes and 17 seats. The KSS, with 2.73% (78,419 votes) and other right-wing groups did not make it into Parliament.[34] This period is characterized by the disintegration and intense polarization of Slovak politics, which had its source in the confrontation policy of HZDS's leader Vladimir Mečiar. The government was formed in the minimum winning coalition format. The hitherto cooperation of the wide-range nationalist HZDS (which presented itself as a popular movement integrating the Christian, social, and national pillar) and the nationalist SNS would not result in a parliamentary majority. For this reason, and after the rejection of SDĽ and KDH, the coalition from Mečiar's second government (November 10, 1993–March 15, 1994) was extended by ZRS, a new and radical-leftist socialist party. Although he resisted joining the government, the leader (and a former member of SDĽ) of this party Ján Ľupták used this empty space to boost its coalition potential. The resulting situation, however, further emphasized the dominant mečiarism vs. antimečiarism (political liberalism vs. authoritarianism) and nationalistic cleavage in the Slovak party system. The creation of the minimum winning coalition with a majority of 83 MPs in the 150-seat Parliament led to the formation of a stable government, which for the first time in the post-1989 history managed to rule for the entire duration of the four-year term.

The government was composed of 18 members, with HZDS populating 12 ministries (apart from the prime minister post, it populated 12 additional ministries such as Ministry of Foreign Affairs, Ministry of Finance, Ministry of the Interior, Ministry of Social Affairs, Ministry of Industry and

---

32 The members of the nationalistic non-parliamentary formation Slovak National Unity SNJ appeared on the bottom of its ballot.
33 Since this was a preelection coalition of four parties, Common Choice had to exceed the 10% threshold, which it managed only narrowly.
34 Statistical Office of the Slovak Republic [on line 25.4.2019]. Available on http://volby.statistics.sk/nrsr/nrsr1994/slov/volby22.htm.

Trade, and Ministry of Agriculture), ZRS 4 ministries (Ministry of Justice) and SNS 2 ministries (Ministry of Defense and Ministry of Education). The importance of ZRS for the formation of the coalition was also confirmed on the executive level, and this party was overrepresented given the total number of mandates in the Parliament. The proportion of its parliamentary mandates and ministerial posts was 15.7%: 22% In the case of SNS, the proportion was balanced, and HZDS was underrepresented on the executive level (73.5%:66,7%) (Balík, Havlík, et al., 2011: 212).

The question is to what extent this was an ideologically homogeneous coalition. Some sources state that especially given the generally declared ideological distance between the far-right and nationalist SNS (Kopeček, 2007: 436–439) and the extreme leftist and socialist ZRS,[35] this should be an ideologically and programmatically heterogeneous coalition.[36] However, other authors point out that if mečiarsim vs. antimečiarism is taken as a fundamental cleavage in the Slovak party system, which caused some parties such as SDĽ and KDH to even refuse to enter the government, we can view this government as ideologically connected (Balík, Havlík, et al. 2011: 199) with certain reservations (e.g., regarding privatization).

However, when using the data obtained by the CMP method, we find that the third government of Vladimír Mečiar does not show huge programmatic differences between the government parties based on the ideological position of these parties in the coalition (which is calculated by taking the difference between the rightist and leftist themes in the programs of the respective parties). This fact is all the more interesting because HZDS and ZRS represented the extreme poles within the ideological profiling of the parliamentary parties. The statement that the coalition was not programmatically homogeneous according to the RILE index is also supported by the fact that the variable range of the parliamentary parties lowered to a value of 14.72 in the RILE index in comparison with 1992 (24.93). This fact is paradoxical in the sense that the verbal rivalry and animosity of the individual leaders of the parties, in particular with regard to Mečiar's confrontational style of politics, began to escalate in this period.

---

35 For the closeness of Workers' Association of Slovakia and Communist Party of Slovakia on the extreme left, see, for example, Kopeček, 2007: 243.
36 Conf. mainly the ideological and programmatic orientation of SNS and ZRS during this government (Kopeček, 2007: 436–442; 231–235).

Table RILE index of the parliamentary parties in the 1994 elections

HZDS	2.66
DÚ	2.40
SNS	-1.54
MK	-5.80
KDH	-6.79
SV	-11.32
ZRS	-12.06
Variable range of the parliamentary parties and their programs	14.72
Turnout	75.65%
Programmatic differences of the HZDS, SNS, ZRS coalition	14.72

See: Manifesto Project. Social Science Research Center Berlin [on line 25.4.2019]. Available on https://visuals.manifesto-project.wzb.eu/mpdb-shiny/cmp_dashboard_dataset/

Chart: Ideological positioning of the parties in 1994 according to the RILE index

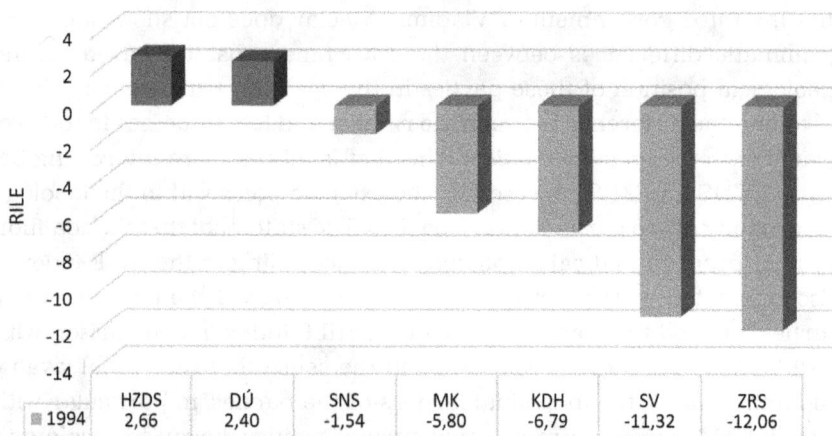

	HZDS	DÚ	SNS	MK	KDH	SV	ZRS
■ 1994	2,66	2,40	-1,54	-5,80	-6,79	-11,32	-12,06

The resulting position of HZDS on the RILE socio-economic scale is 2.66 as in the coalition (thence the centrist position of this party with a slight predominance of rightist topics). Paradoxically, we get a negative value of -1.54 with SNS, which indicates the centrist nature of SNS's program objectives, with a slight predominance of leftist themes. These program data therefore do not correspond at all with the rhetoric, practical decisions, and perception of SNS as an extremely right-wing nationalist party. The Association of Workers of Slovakia, a party that presented itself through leftist topics and borderline socialist rhetoric, scored adequately at -12.06, that is, the preponderance of leftist political agenda was evident in its program.[37] The actual program range of the minimum winning coalition of HZDS, SNS, and ZRS (with the program score of 100 to -100) was slightly shifted to the left, and it was relatively ideologically connected given its relatively low programmatic differences at 14.72 between the centrist program of HZDS and the leftist agenda of ZRS. In addition to HZDS, which defined itself as a centrist formation, even ZRS made good to its widespread leftist image – a party looking into the interests of blue-collar workers.

The problem of this coalition, however, was mainly the exercise of power: with marginalization of opposition parties and their supervisory duties in Parliament, as well as with unconstitutional decisions of the government and the ruling majority in the Parliament, which were more than once identified by the Constitutional Court of the Slovak Republic (ÚS SR).[38] Particularly because of the ways how power was exercised,[39] the Slovak political system was deeply intertwined by the conflict line between the supporters and opponents of V. Mečiar – the so-called mečiarism vs. antimečiarism (or political liberalism vs. authoritarianism). Its intensity was so strong that it became an obstacle to the consolidation of democratic institutions during the term of office of the HZDS, SNS, and ZRS, and it overshadowed other conflicts such as church-state, communism-anticommunism, and the socio-economic transformation line. On the other hand, this specific conflict line partially correlated with the urban-rural cleavage because the voters of the majority parties were generally from smaller towns and rural areas. The illiberal exercise of power of the third coalition government of

---

37 The opposition parties, such as SV, reached a level of -11.32, that is, they were leaning to the left, and to a lesser extent, this was also the case with KDH (-6.79) and MK (-5.69). Only DÚ with 2.40 appeared as a party in the center-right part of the spectrum (or liberal) in terms of the program objectives and the difference between the rightist and leftist party themes. The data are based on the Manifesto Project, Social Science Research Center Berlin [on line 25.4.2019]. Available on https://visuals.manifesto-project.wzb.eu/mpdb-shiny/cmp_dashboard_dataset/.

38 The revocation of František Gaulieder's MP mandate for HZDS, labeling of the formation of parliamentary investigation committees as unconstitutional, findings confirming the unconstitutional nature of fundamental privatization laws in 1994–1996, unconstitutional nature of amendments to the electoral law from 1998, marring of the referendum on the direct presidential elections by the government in 1997, etc. (Bútora, Ivantyšyn, et al., 1998: 45).

39 As a result of the unconstitutional governmental decisions, the Slovak Republic was excluded from the so-called Luxembourg Group of countries, which were involved in the 1997 accession negotiations to join the EU.

Vladimír Mečiar (HZDS, SNS, and ZRS), which led to the violations of liberal principles on the horizontal level of exercise of power together with a non-transparent privatization of the state assets, has created the foundations for the current influence of business and oligarchic structures in Slovakia. The lacking political control by the former opposition, the public, and the media over the partisan redistribution of state property led to the formation of illiberal democracy and/or authoritarian practices of corporate governance. These circumstances led to the exclusion of the Slovak Republic from the European and transatlantic integration. This political development gradually created public pressure on the closer cooperation of the opposition parties KDH, DU, and DS, which agreed to coordinate their activities in the so-called Blue Coalition. The institutional cooperation later led to the necessary integration of the opposition parties into a general preelection coalition under the name SDK. This was formed by the right-wing parties KDH, DÚ, and DS and the leftist SDSS and SZS. Its aim was to stop the destruction of liberal-democratic institutions vis-a-vis the centralization of power at the level of executive government and the prime minister and disrespect for the basic principles of constitutionalism and the rule of law. This regime met the requirements for an illiberal democracy by polarizing the society with the style of governance of the then Prime Minister Vladimír Mečiar, increasing populist and nationalist rhetoric, erosion of the principles of horizontal separation of powers, criminalization of the opposition, cooperation of public security forces with organized criminal groups, constant search for internal enemy of the state, corruption in the privatization of state property, censorship of critics and government propaganda in the public media, ad hoc adjustments to the electoral or other laws, for example, in the selection of the Director of the Slovak Information Service etc.

With respect to the above development problems, the RILE index does not show huge programmatic differences in the period since 1994 between the said coalition government parties (HZDS, SNS, and ZRS). At a first glance, this coalition appears to be ideologically heterogeneous due to the presence of the nationalist HZDS and SNS[40] and the socialist ZRS. In view of the ongoing process of economic transformation, rising unemployment and limited welfare, it is not all too surprising that majority of the parliamentary parties sided with the leftist and social themes in 1994. This fact is also confirmed by the RILE indexes of the parliamentary parties.

---

40 On the strengthening of the nationalist-traditional wing in HZDS after 1992, see Kopeček, 2007: 160.

An interesting feature is that such parties also included the conservative-nationalist parties such as SNS and KDH based on the RILE index. This fact reflects the worsening economic situation of the population compared to 1992 where the rightist and rightist-centrist programs prevailed among the parliamentary parties.

The structure of the electoral programs also includes some fundamentally common characteristics. The most obvious ones within the framework of the parliamentary parties include the need for development of a democratic political system, unemployment solutions, and, particularly, a more efficient social system. Since the ZRS only marginally included some of the observed topics into its program or avoided them completely, we conclude that the other parties agreed on the streamlining of public administration, social policy, education, and health and making decisions about the performance of other economic reforms in their programs. These would therefore potentially represent the so-called valence topics, which the ruling parties agreed to address. All parties required the solutions in welfare support, creation of new jobs, and the need to reduce unemployment. All parties also declared the need for the development of democratic institutions.

The extreme ideological position of the ZRS was also reflected in the fact that without this party in the Parliament (and, subsequently, in the government), the intersection and overlap of topics among the parliamentary parties would further increase since the HZDS, KDH, and SNS, and also KDH, DÚ, and MK had a similar approach to the foreign, economic, and cultural relations, the reform of territorial and local governments; decentralization; support for the development of scientific and research projects, sports activities, youth; health care (improved availability and efficient funding); promotion of sustainable development; tourism and the state support of small and medium business.

The quasi-valency themes are represented by a more numerous category, and similar to the valency themes, the ZRS program is visibly different from the other parties. The overlap of ZRS with the rest of the parliamentary parties is particularly in the quasi-valency topics such as the support of economic growth (investments in housing and road infrastructure), reform of social policy, status and salaries of the teachers, low inflation rates, and fight against corruption.

The most obvious positioning theme, which divided the parliamentary parties, was the issue of privatization of state property, its continuation, methods, and nature. This was the most polarizing element on the political scene across the entire political spectrum. The differences between the members of the coalition could be observed even in this topic. HZDS supported privatization, but stressed the need to maintain the state majority in the privatized sectors such as energy, gas, transport, and telecommunications. An ambiguous position was presented by SNS, which on the one hand refused the privatization and sale of state assets to foreign corporations, that is, it preferred the Slovak "national" bodies through the sale of businesses to the Slovak business groups. On the other hand, however, its program mentions privatization, particularly in the field of economy. ZRS did not encourage the privatization of state property at all.[41] It follows from the above that the individual coalition parties had their own approaches to this issue; however, their attitude was different from the attitude of other opposition parties: DÚ, KDH, and MK (with the exception of Common Choice – SV). In line with their leftist program, the coalition of parties under the name Common Choice (-11.32 on the RILE scale) opposed the continuation of privatization of the state property.

The second positioning theme across the parliamentary spectrum, which visibly differentiated some parties in the coalition and opposition, was education – SMK and MK took a different approach to the development of education. While SNS accentuated the need for instruction to be provided in the national language, which was, according to SNS, a precondition for the development of patriotism and national integrity, the Hungarian Coalition (MK) stressed a broader autonomy of the Hungarian minority even in the context of education being provided in the minority mother tongue. Its program also included decentralization, which would promote the creation of higher territorial units based on the historical regions, which would further foster the development of greater cultural autonomy of ethnic minorities. Other parties took a less strong position in relation to the above topics, they rejected the solution of educational reforms with decentralization and nationalist tools, and stressed the principles of civic pluralism in a democratic society (SV, HZDS, and DÚ).

In terms of the topical structure and following the CMP methodology, which categorizes the topics into core areas (social groups, social order, welfare and quality of life, economy, political system, freedom and democ-

---

41 The Workers' Association of Slovakia (ZRS) with its head Ján Ľupták launched a petition at the end of 1993, which resulted in a parliamentary referendum in June concerning the law on proving the origin of proceeds from auctions and privatization. On October 22, 1994, a referendum with the question Do you agree that a law on proving the origin of proceeds from the auctions and privatization should be passed? was held. The turnout was only 19.96% and the referendum did not meet the necessary constitutional majority quorum to be considered valid.

racy, and international relations), all parliamentary parties predominant-
ly supported "welfare and quality of life," ranging from the programmatically most rightist program of HZDS (31.23%) through the leftist program
of KDH (39.51%), which had the largest share in this topic, to the program
of SV (where this topic was represented at 35.85%). ZRS stands out in the
comparison of RILE and CMP. This party won the extreme left position
(-12.06) in the RILE index in the Slovak party system. However, when analyzing its topics, we can conclude that ZRS paid the least attention (of just
2.13%) to "welfare and quality of life," which dominated in the structure of
themes presented by other parties. The program of this extremely leftist
party was dominated by the "social groups" theme, with a score of 48.94%.
This made it significantly different from the other parties where "welfare
and quality of life" prevailed. The parties where "welfare and the quality
of life" dominated in 1994 also included DÚ (30.70%) and SNS (31.12%). With
MK, the proportion of its program in this area was the second lowest (i.e.,
at a level of 18.26%).

Parliamentary Elections in 1998

The return to the European states with a real ambition to integrate into
the EU and NATO structures presupposed the creation of real political
alternatives against the ruling coalition HZDS, SNS, and ZRS (1994–1998).
The only short-term strategy that would allow the opposition parties to
implement this goal was a wider integration of smaller opposition parties.
This began to take shape by combining three right-centrist parties: KDH,
DÚ, and DS. The so-called Blue Coalition was formed at the end of 1996.
One of the reasons of the said inter-party cooperation and the later integration of the opposition parties into the project, which also included the
leftist parties SDSS and SZS, was the kidnapping of the president's son
Michal Kováč jr. (allegedly organized by the Slovak Information Service)
and the thwarted referendum on the direct election of the president and
entry into NATO, which took place on May 23 and 24, 1997. This resulted in
a more intense cooperation of the opposition parties and the subsequent
creation of a broad preelection coalition bearing the name "Slovak Democratic Coalition" (SDK). SDK, headed by its speaker and leader Mikuláš
Dzurinda, was an ideologically heterogeneous group of parties. Its primary
goal was to reverse the political developments in Slovakia toward the con-

solidation of democratic institutions and integration into the Euro-Atlantic structures. The mečiarism vs. antimečiarism cleavage, which divided the parties and society at large, was consequently supplemented by the "European integration" topic in the 1998 elections. The subsequent amendment of the electoral law of 1998, which established the 5% the threshold for each party in the preelection coalition, was also responded to by the parties in the Hungarian minority coalition. The parties freely associated in the MK created a new political Party of the Hungarian Coalition Magyar Koalíció Pártja (SMK). Due to the targeted modifications of the electoral law by the then ruling coalition of HZDS, SNS, and ZRS, the parties of the preelection coalition SDK had to formally integrate and register themselves as a standalone party.

The elections held on September 25 and 26, 1998, were affected by the efforts to intensify the integration processes in the Euro-Atlantic structures, but also by the topics related to the political system, development of democracy, reform of the rule of law, freedoms and human rights, security etc. The elections were preceded by massive civil mobilization since most of the mass media, with the exception of Radio Twist and several national dailies and the new private TV Markíza, were influenced by the government-controlled media such as the Slovak Radio and Slovak Television. Despite the ban on election campaigns in the private media, the increased civic mobilization was also reflected in electoral turnout. It reached 84.24% of all eligible voters, and compared to the 1994 elections (75.65%) it rose by 8.59%. Mečiar's HZDS won the elections with 27% (907,103 votes) (43 seats), however, the government was formed by the parties of the antimečiar opposition. This was thanks to the cooperation and integration of the opposition parties into the SDK, emergence of yet another political party in Parliament, and the ruling ZRS not exceeding the necessary 5% support. After all the ballots were turned in, the opposition parties won the constitutional majority, which was necessary to change the constitution and fill the empty presidential post (March 2, 1998). The change of the constitutional law and introduction of direct presidential elections was fostered by the political developments. The reason for this was the fact that after the end of Michal Kováč's term, some of the responsibilities were passed onto the government and prime minister. This further strengthened the executive branch to the detriment of other components of power. For this reason, the introduction of direct election of the president became a major positioning theme between the parties of the then ruling coalition and the antimečiar opposition. The Party of the SDK won 26.33% (884,497) of the votes in the 1998 elections and it occupied 42 mandates, followed by SDĽ with 14.66%

(492,507 votes) and 23 seats, SMK with 9.12% (306,623 votes) and 15 seats, SNS with 9.07% (304 839 votes) and 14 seats and SOP with 8.01% (269,343 votes) and 13 seats in the NR SR. Given the number of relevant parties in the Parliament, which also grew due to the real preelection coalition SDK (which was only a formal group), we can conclude that the fragmentation of the political system has increased at the parliamentary level. Even entirely new parties such as SOP made it into Parliament.

On the other hand, the 5% election clause became an obstacle for the extreme right-wing Slovak National Unity, which only won 0.13% (4688 votes) and the Slovak People's Party with 0.27% (9227 votes). On the left, the Association of Workers of Slovakia with 1.30% (43,809 votes) and the KSS with 2.79% (94,015 votes) remained outside Parliament.[42]

In this period, the reduction of variable tensions in the party system did not lead to extreme right-wing and left-wing parties making it into Parliament. One of the causes of the above situation was the ability of the parliamentary parties (at high turnouts and thanks to the political polarization between the parties) to reach most of the voters, and the fragmentation of the radical extremist bodies, which caused the dispersion of constituency of these parties and their subsequent political marginalization.

After the 1998 elections, the Slovak party system was polarized, especially between the hitherto coalition and opposition parties representing two different political blocs, which also differed in political priorities.[43] This situation was not even affected by the emergence of the broad coalition government of SDK, SDĽ, SMK, and SOP. The reason for this was the fact that the SDK was founded on the basis of the preelection cooperation of five parties and SMK was established from three parties of the Hungarian minority whose integration was accelerated by changes in the electoral system, which disfavored preelection coalitions. Together with SDĽ and SOP, the government in actuality consisted of 10 parties. At the beginning of its term, this coalition had a constitutional majority of 93 parliamentary seats. The coalition agreement was formally signed on October 28, 1998. In the first government of Mikuláš Dzurinda, the representatives of individual parties were represented evenly based on their mandates in the Parliament. An exception was the SOP, which only managed two ministries despite the fact that it won 14% of the mandates in the context of the co-

---

42 Statistical Office of the Slovak Republic [on line 25.4.2019]. Available on http://volby.statistics.sk/nrsr/nrsr1998/results/tab2.jsp.htm.
43 The two-bloc party system within the context of the Slovak political party system was characterized by Leška (2013: 34) in the relevant phase.

alition parties. This disproportion, however, was compensated for in the subsequent presidential elections, where the SOP party leader becomes a government candidate for the presidential post. The overrepresentation of the ministers was also evident with SDĽ, which won a 30% share of representation in the government and six ministries (e.g., Ministry of Finance, Ministry of Defense, Ministry of Social Affairs, and Ministry of Agriculture). This situation was tolerated by the other coalition partners despite the fact that its percentage of coalition seats in Parliament only amounted to 24.1%. SDK and SMK were represented proportionally to their parliamentary seats and other coalition partners (45.2%: 45%) (16,1%: 15%).[44]

The conditions for the consolidation of democratic institutions in Slovakia were therefore based on the coalition, which is often characterized as broad and ideologically heterogeneous (Balík, Havlík, et al., 2011: 202). It was based on the majority-opposition parties from the years 1994–1998.

The programmatic differences of the broad constitutional coalition (12.33 on the RILE scale), however, was lower than the one in third Mečiar's government (14.72). Thus, it is questionable to what extent can this government coalition be seen as ideologically heterogeneous if its members exhibited a closer programmatic homogeneity in the right-left ideological continuum than Čarnogurský's minimum winning government VPN, KDH, DS (with a programmatic span of 32.05) or Mečiar's minimum winning ideologically connected coalition HZDS, SNS, and ZRS. If we only based our assumptions on quantifiable data from the programs of the said government parties and coalitions in the context of the RILE scale, even the first Dzurinda's wide coalition could be characterized as oversized, ideologically connected and therefore homogeneous. Otherwise, if we base our assumptions on the definition of the positioning value within the right-left continuum, we would have to reevaluate the earlier mentioned characteristics of government coalitions, especially Ján Čarnogurský's, which ruled in the period 1990–1992 and consisted of VPN, KDH, and DS, and showed substantially broader programmatic differences on the RILE scale.

The variable range between the two extreme parties in the party system according to the RILE index, however, grew from the original 14.72 in 1994 to 21.04 in 1998. This figure correlates with the general development toward a more intense political polarization of the party system.

---

44 See Balík, Havlík, et al. 2011: 212.

Table RILE index of the parliamentary parties in the 1998 elections

SNS	13.86
SDK	5.19
HZDS	0.75
SDĽ	-6.25
SOP	-6.39
SMK	-7.18
Variable range of the parliamentary parties and their programs	21.04
Turnout	84.24%
Programmatic differences in the SDK, SDĽ, SMK, SOP coalition	12.33

See: Manifesto Project. Social Science Research Center Berlin [on line 25.4.2019]. Available on https://visuals.manifesto-project.wzb.eu/mpdb-shiny/cmp_dashboard_dataset/

Chart: Ideological positioning of the parties in 1998 according to the RILE index

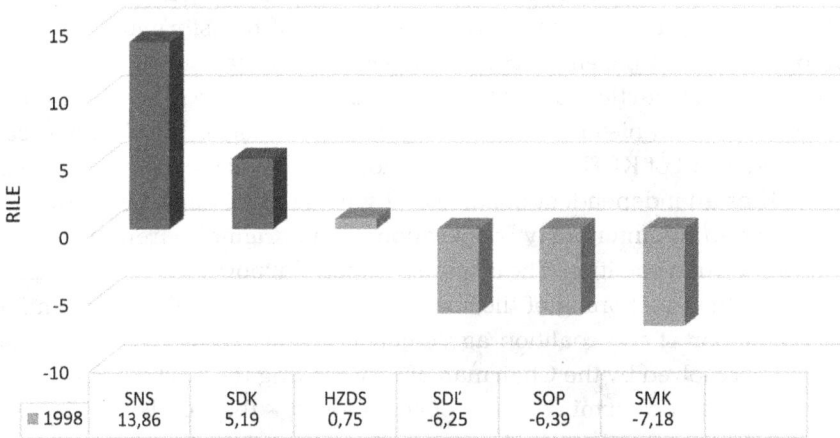

	SNS	SDK	HZDS	SDĽ	SOP	SMK
1998	13,86	5,19	0,75	-6,25	-6,39	-7,18

The biggest programmatic shift in the 1998 parliamentary elections can be observed with SNS. This party moved from the leftist-centrist position of -1.54 in 1994 to the right, and to the very edge of the right spectrum with 13.86 on the RILE scale. Other parties have exhibited smaller shifts. The HZDS shifted slightly to the center from 2.66 in 1994 to 0.75 in 1998. Similarly, the centrist status of SDĽ changed: as a central party in the SV preelection coalition in 1994, it moved from -11.32 to the political center with a value of 6.25 on the RILE scale. The SMK, which was formed on the basis of previous collaboration of MK in 1994, has moved in the opposite direction: slightly to the left from -5.80 to -7.18 in 1998. This shift meant that it became an extremely leftist party in the system of Slovak parliamentary parties in 1998.

The reason for the lower degree of ideological differences between the parties of the first Dzurinda's government was also the common objectives in the domestic and foreign policy of the country. Its aim was to eliminate the democratic deficits in the national institutions, accelerate the economic transformation, and negotiate the terms for entry into the EU and NATO. In the context of the broad constitutional coalition of Prime Minister Mikuláš Dzurinda, however, the existing valency topics (foreign policy, reform of the political system, expansion of freedom and human rights, development of infrastructure, reduction of unemployment, promotion of economic growth, regional support, social policy, education, health, environment, etc.) were also accompanied by positioning topics. Within these, the most visible conflict formed in determining the strategy for privatization of the state property and tax policies. This conflict escalated especially among the representatives of SDK and SDĽ. The standard political intra-coalition disputes were also revolving around the issue of transformation of SDK into the original parent parties. This dispute between the leaders of the former parent parties escalated between the then Prime Minister Mikuláš Dzurinda and Minister of Justice of the Slovak Republic Ján Čarnogurský (the then head of KDH). Mikuláš Dzurinda advocated for the preservation of SDK as an independent political entity, while Ján Čarnogurský wanted to return to the inter-party cooperation of the original parent parties in the preelection coalition. The dispute between Čarnogurský and Dzurinda changed the functioning of the coalition, and in 2000, KDH became a formal member of the coalition agreement (Kopeček, 2007: 111). The situation was resolved by the Chairman of SDK leaving the party with a group of members and forming a new political party – the SDKÚ in February 2000. The need for the establishment of a constitutional and broad coalition after 1998, however, damaged the image of the left-wing SDĽ. Since the beginning of Dzurinda's first government, this party had reservations concerning the creation of constitutional majority with the ethnically oriented SMK. This fact demonstrates the persistence of the nationalist cleavage in Slovak politics and it created tensions in the ruling coalition. Since the first Vice-President of SDĽ Robert Fico with the highest number of preferential votes (194,519) wasn't awarded any major government office within the framework of SDĽ, he became the biggest coalition critic of the then government. Then, in the second half of 1999, he left the party and founded

SMER. In 2000, the Democratic Union integrated into the structures of the newly established SDKÚ and the other parties in the former SDK coalition such as SDSS and SZS returned to the position of politically independent but marginal players.

The leftist SMER presented itself not only as an alternative to Mečiar's HZDS, but also the governing SDĽ and SDKÚ. The inner crisis in SDĽ culminated in 2002 by the departure of one of the reforming fractions in this social-democratic party. Its supporters subsequently formed a new party – the Social Democratic Alternative (SDA). A similar process of gradual decline was also typical for the new parliamentary party SOP. In accordance with the new constitutional law on direct election of the president, its party leader and founder Rudolf Schuster ran for president for the ruling coalition in the upcoming presidential elections. With 57.18% of the votes in the second round (i.e., 1,727,481 ballots)[45], Rudolf Schuster became the first directly elected president of the Slovak Republic. In the second round of the presidential elections, he defeated Vladimír Mečiar who won 1,293,642 votes, that is, 42.82% of the votes. Even these presidential elections confirmed the stabilization of the mečiarism vs. antimečiarism cleavage in Slovak politics. The social-democratic SOP, however, lost its most prominent public figure (Rudolf Schuster) for president, it failed to overcome the charismatic-crony development phase, and the departure of Rudolf Schuster subsequently caused a period of instability in the party and undermined its public support.

The ideological diversity of all antimečiar bodies was the main cause of an extensive fragmentation of the party system in the years 1998–2002. The development of the party system in this period, however, signaled a shift from the hitherto dominant mečiarism vs. antimečiarism cleavage to the standard socioeconomic and urban-rural cleavage. The parties gradually began to define themselves on the RILE axis. The specific cleavage of mečiarism vs. antimečiarism had a particular impact on the parties representing the interests of the Hungarian minority in Slovakia. The presence of nationalist rhetoric and nationalist cleavage in the party system[46] meant that the originally centrist and leftist parties (ESWMK with a RILE index of 5,26 in 1990, MKM-EGY with a RILE index of 5,26 in 1992, MK with a RILE index of -5,69 in 1994, and SMK with a RILE index of -7,18 in 1998),

---

45 For more information on the disintegration of parties in the antimečiar bloc, see Kopeček, 2006: 198–202.
46 Especially HZDS and SNS, and SDĽ and SMK to a lesser degree, were the bearers of the nationalist themes in the political discourse.

which represented the interests of the Hungarian-speaking population in the southern rural regions of Slovakia, became unusual (in a normally functioning party system) political and coalition partners of the rightist parties in the period of search for an internal enemy of independent Slovakia particularly during the third Mečiar's government (1994–1998). This was evidenced by the coalition cooperation in the first and second Dzurinda's government (1998–2002; 2002–2006). This cooperation was later renewed in Iveta Radičová's government in 2010–2012. The party system fragmented even further in the period 1998–2002. This process also included the breakup of the opposition SNS (Kopeček, 2007: 428–433), departures of other key politicians from HZDS,[47] and the divisions in SDĽ[48]. In view of the sheer number of parties in Parliament, the party system maintained the position of extreme pluralism with ideological polarization between the ruling and opposition parties (i.e., polarized pluralism with a high degree of fragmentation of the party system).

Despite the fact that the broad coalition with the social-democratic SDĽ and SOP on one side of the spectrum and the conservative Christian-democratic KDH, SDKÚ, and ethno-regional SMK on the other led to a number of governmental disputes in the years 1998–2002; the coalition remained functional and stable until the next ordinary parliamentary elections in 2002.

Parliamentary Elections in 2002

In the regular elections held on September 20–21, 2002, altogether seven parties made it into Parliament and the voter turnout reached 70.06% of the eligible voters. The originally centrist HZDS with 19.5% (560,691 votes) received 36 mandates, the christian-rightist SDKÚ with 15.09% (433,953 votes) received 28 seats, the SMER with 13.46% (387,100 votes) received 25 seats (an attempt at the third way following the model of the British laborist Tony Blair), the ethnic coalition SMK with 11.17% won 20 seats, the Christian-conservative KDH with 8.25% (237,202 votes) received 15 seats and the liberal Alliance of the New Citizen with 8.01% (230,309 votes) won 15 seats.

---

47 For more, see Kopeček, 2007: 168–172.
48 For more, see Kopeček, 2007: 199–200.

Surprisingly, even the KSS made it into Parliament [49] with 6.33% (181,872 votes) and 11 seats.[50]

Although HZDS won most of the votes (19.5%), its minimum coalition potential and the polarization of the party system it participated in left it in isolation and unable to form a government. This was also caused by the fact that the HZDS's previously traditional opposition and nationalist co-alition partner SNS in the years 1998–2002 split into SNS and the Original Slovak National Party (PSNS).[51]

Due to the division of the original constituency, both parties did not make it into Parliament. The PSNS won 3.65% (105,084) of the votes and the SNS won 3.32% (95,633) of the votes. Apart from the nationalist SNS and PSNS, even the social-democratic SDĽ with 1.36% (39,163 votes) and the leftist SDA, which split off from SDĽ, with 1.79% (51,649 votes) did not make it into Parliament. The same applied to the HZDS departees led by Ivan Gašparovič, who founded the Movement for Democracy (HZD) with 3.28% (94,324 votes): they did not exceed the 5% threshold for entry into Parliament. A similar drop in the votes was recorded with the extreme right-wing and non-parliamentary parties such as the People's Party (ĽS) with 0.02% (763 votes) and Slovak National Unity with 0.15% (4,548 votes).

The second cabinet of Mikuláš Dzurinda was based on the coalition cooperation of the rightist-centrist SDKÚ, SMK, KDH, and the newly established Alliance of the New Citizen (ANO). The coalition was of a minimum winning kind, with a narrow majority of 78 seats in the 150-seat Parliament.

---

49 The Communist Party of Slovakia (KSS) was formed in 1992 in a merger of the KSS '91 and the Union of Communists of Slovakia, which separated from SDĽ in 1991. The party adhered to the marxist-leninist principles and rejected the entry into the Euro-Atlantic structures.

50 Statistical Office of the Slovak Republic [on line 25.4.2019]. Available on http://volby.statistics.sk/nrsr/nrsr2002/webdata/vysledky_a.htm.

51 The Original SNS originated from an internal dispute about the style of leadership in SNS. Ján Slota became its leader. The reason for this division was Anna Malíková's efforts (new head of SNS in the period September 25, 1999–May 31, 2003) to push out Ján Slota's sympathizers from major and electable positions in the party. The reasons behind the efforts to marginalize Ján Slota and his sympathizers were the cases of corruption, personal scandals, and the confrontational style of SNS policies under Ján Slota's leadership. His followers subsequently decided to become independent and established the rightist Original SNS (October 6, 2001). This schism and the absence of both nationalist parties in Parliament in the years 2002–2006 led the representatives of SNS and PSNS to renegotiate the merger of these parties. The parties have merged under the name SNS on April 30, 2003. After the unification congress, Ján Slota once again became head of the party. In the subsequent parliamentary elections in 2006, SNS won 11.73% of the votes and yet again, it became not only a parliamentary but also a ruling party in the coalition with SMER-SD and HZDS-ĽS.

The representation of the individual parties in the government reflected the proportion of parliamentary seats, with only SDKÚ having a slight overrepresentation since the share of coalition mandates in the Parliament (35.9%) corresponded to 37.5% of the mandates in the government.[52] In most politological analyses, the coalition presented itself as more programmatically homogeneous than the first cabinet of M. Dzurinda (Kopeček, 2007: 113), compare (Balík, Havlík, et al., 2011: 203) and the third government of V. Mečiar. However, how does this finding correspond to the distribution of ideological orientations of the parties according to the RILE index?

Table RILE index of the parliamentary parties in the 2002 elections

SDKÚ	37.28
KDH	27.19
HZDS	20.63
ANO	18.58
SMER	8,86
SMK	-0.60
KSS	-7.14
Variable range of the parliamentary parties and their programs	44.5
Turnout	70.07%
Programmatic differences in the SDKÚ,SMK, KDH, and ANO coalition	37.96

Source: Manifesto Project. Social Science Research Center Berlin [on line 25.4.2019]. Available on https://visuals.manifesto-project.wzb.eu/mpdb-shiny/cmp_dashboard_dataset/

Despite the programmatic proximity of the parties, in particular in the economic area, the RILE index shows an increase in the ideological differences between the parties. This phenomenon is manifested in the emerging ruling coalition in Dzurinda's second government, but also in the parliamentary parties. The variable range of the programs in the party system almost doubled from 21.04 to 44.5. The reason is the visible shift in the SDKÚ program as a successor of SDK, in particular from the position of a centrist-rightist party, that is, with a score of 5.15, into the extreme right with 37.36 points in the RILE index. A similar shift can be seen with KDH,

---

52 For more, see (Balík, Havlík, et al. 2011: 212).

Chart: Ideological positioning of the parties in 2002 according to the RILE index

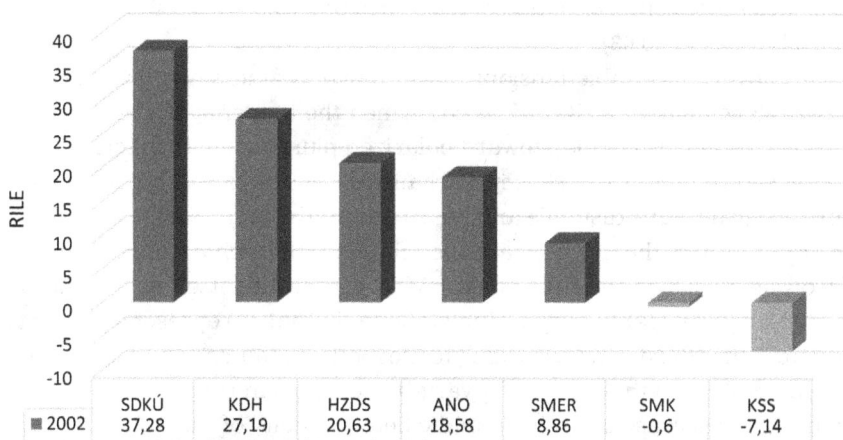

	SDKÚ	KDH	HZDS	ANO	SMER	SMK	KSS
■ 2002	37,28	27,19	20,63	18,58	8,86	-0,6	-7,14

which assumed a centrist-left position with -6.79 in 1994, but took a turn for the right in 2002 with key rightist values and a score of 27.19. In general, most parties moved to the right in this election year. This tendency is especially true for the hitherto centrist HZDS, which acted as a centrist party in the Slovak Parliament in 1994 (RILE index of 2.66) and in 1998 (RILE index of 0.75) not just rhetorically but also programmatically. In the elections of 2002, however, their program scored at 20.63 on the RILE scale, that is, it was rightist (just below KDH with 27.19 and SDKÚ with 37.36, which represented the extreme right position in the right-wing range). Similar to KDH and SDKÚ, even the newly established party ANO, founded by Pavol Rusko, an entrepreneur and co-owner of a private TV broadcast Markíza, showed the correlation between its programmatic orientation and presentation as a liberal party with a value of 18.49 on the RILE scale.

Despite the substantial shift to the right (even in the context of SMK, which transformed from the leftist value of -7.18 (in 1998) to a centrist position of -0.60 (in 2002), the polarization of the party system was offset and balanced by the entry of the KSS into Parliament. The KSS took a position in the extreme left of the spectrum with a score of -7.14. In actuality, this corresponds to the level of a moderate leftist-centrist party. Its onset was aided by the disintegration of the left (SDĽ, SDA, SDSS, etc.) and transition of the voters of these parties to other bodies, such as SMER. Even this party rhetorically declared its left-liberal position in the political spectrum. The entry of KSS into Parliament filled the absence of leftist and social-democratic bodies in the Slovak Parliament. At the same time, and aided by the SDKÚ's shift to the right, it caused the ideological polarization and ideological differentiation of the opposition (the opposition HZDS with a RILE index of 20.63).

The overall variable tensions of the party system since 1998 (21.04 on the RILE scale) rose to 44.5. This confirmed the tendency of the party system in Slovakia to develop toward polarized pluralism both in terms of the increased number of parties in Parliament (7) and increasing ideological and programmatic distance and polarization. The value and programmatic orientation of the newly established SMER with its charismatic leader R. Fico was at 8.86 on the RILE scale. SMER established itself as a moderate centrist-rightist party despite the statements that it represents the "new left" and the "third way" according to the model of the British Labour Party.

In addition to the increasing variable tensions in the party system, we can see an increase of programmatic heterogeneity of the ruling coalition in the RILE index despite the fact that this coalition is usually described as "relatively homogeneous" (Kopeček, 2007: 113) and ideologically connected. The variable tensions of the coalition in Dzurinda's second cabinet paradoxically rose from 12.33 in his first broad coalition (SDK, SDĽ, SMK, and SOP) to 37.96. This fact was not prevented by the wide consensus on the fundamental economic objectives of the government such as finalizing the privatization process of strategic energy companies. Despite these important valence or quasi-valence themes that joined the parties in the ruling coalition, the instability of the government appeared in the area of culture and values. The conflict between the coalition and opposition parties from the very inception of government on October 16, 2002, indicates a partial standardization of the party system on the right-to-left ideological scale (except for HZDS and SMK). On the other hand, the party competition gave way to yet another standard cleavage in the party system: state-church. This formed a new positioning theme among the very parties in the ruling coalition. Conflicts between the conservative KDH and liberal ANO in the minimum winning coalition also emerged in connection with the hitherto marginal topics. Especially at the beginning of the term when the government was being formed, the party system continued to be affected by the mečiarism vs. antimečiarism cleavage because the head of HZDS did not win the support of SDKÚ, KDH, and SMK due to his low level of trust in these parties in the negotiations to form a majority ruling coalition. The creation of a majority government by the right-wing parties also confirmed the consolidation and standard conflict lines even after the emergence of new actants such as ANO, SMER, and KSS in parliamentary politics. On the other hand, the developments did not lead to the elimination of fragmentation of the party system. After the collapse of the ANO parliamentary group, departure of the members of the SDKÚ parliamentary group (Ivan Šimko and Zuzana Martináková) who founded the Free Forum (SF) and the coalition party KDH from the government for a controversy regarding the adoption of the law on reservations in conscience, the early parliamentary elections were held on June 17, 2006.

The low coalition potential of HZDS combined with factors such as the loss of SNS and PSNS mandates resulted in the political isolation of this party in this parliamentary term. This factor was also transformed into the declining intensity of the mečiarism vs. antimečiarism cleavage. This cleavage was gradually replaced by the socio-economic cleavage and the state-church cleavage, which began to differentiate the positioning topics between the ruling and opposition parties. These developments thus created the conditions for consolidating the party system along the standard cleavage lines. Despite this fact, the shaping of the two political blocs of partisan cooperation, which had a source in the second half of the 1990s, still persisted. This fact was reflected not only in the repeated growth of the variable range of the parliamentary parties at 44.5 on the RILE scale (in 1998 the value totaled 21.04), but also in the programmatic differences of the ruling coalition SDKÚ, KDH, ANO, and SMK. All this despite the fact that this coalition is usually labeled as a minimum majority and ideologically connected, with the programmatic differences of 37.96 on the RILE scale. This has meant an increase in the programmatic differences of the coalition parties compared to the first government of Mikuláš Dzurinda (12.33 on the RILE scale) by 25.63 on the RILE scale. For this reason, it is difficult to place this coalition (using the programmatic values of the parties on the RILE scale) among the ideologically homogeneous coalitions when compared, for example, with the first coalition government of Mikuláš Dzurinda (1998–2002), or even with the third Mečiar's cabinet (1994–1998). For this reason, if we follow up on the quantification of the programs of the individual parties on the right-to-left axis, two interpretations are possible. We either place the second Dzurinda's government SDKÚ, KDH, ANO, and SMK among the ideologically connected minimum winning coalitions and readjust the classification of the first Dzurinda's coalition SDK, SDĽ, SMK, and SOP as a broad, supernumerary and therefore constitutional and ideologically homogeneous coalition – or we base our assumptions on the original standpoint: the first government coalition of M. Dzurinda was broad and ideologically heterogeneous (i.e., with the programmatic differences between the ruling parties at 12.33 on the RILE scale), and it already falls into the category of ideologically diverse coalitions. As a result of the adjustments in the perception of the programmatic homogeneity and heterogeneity of the government, and due to a higher variable range of the programs of the governing parties SDKÚ, KDH, SMK, and ANO in 2002 (37.96), we will readjust its classification to a minimum winning but heterogeneous coalition (and also the classification of other government groups since 1990). An exception here is the second cabinet of Vladimír Mečiar (HZDS and SNS) in 1992–1994 with the programmatic differences of the coalition at 1.06 on the RILE scale. This second approach would be too analytical and rigid to assess the programmatic closeness of the political parties in the government, in particular because in most consolidated democracies it is normal for the Christian-democratic, people's and liberal parties to cooperate. Such a cooperation is regarded as politically natural and complementary particularly for the apparent closeness in economic topics. An example of political closeness of these parties can be observed in the consolidated democratic systems such as the Federal Republic of Germany or Kingdom of the Netherlands. In the Federal Republic of Germany, the liberal FDP is considered to be the closest coalition partner of the people's party and the Christian democrats (CDU/CSU).[53]After the collapse of the consociational model in the Kingdom of the Netherlands, the confessional Catholic People's Party (KVP), Protestant Antirevolutionary Party (ARP), and the Christian Historical Union (CHU) integrated into the centrist Christian Democratic Appeal (CDA). This became a close coalition partner of the liberal People's Party for Freedom and Democracy (VVD) in the post-consociational period.[54]

For the above reasons, and in view of the political proximity of the rightist and liberal parties, as well as due to the programmatic span of the rul-

---

53 The cooperation of CDU/CSU with FDP stabilized after 1982. Since then the FDP has been part of all Helmut Kohl's governments until 1999. The gradual penetration and establishment of the environmentally oriented party Bundestag Fraction Alliance 90/The Green Party in the Bundestag since the 1990s were a consequence of the political cooperation with CDU and CSU. Subsequently, FDP became a coalition partner of CDU/CSU even in the second Merkel's cabinet in the years 2010–2014. The only exception was the periods of the broad coalition of SDU/CSU with SPD when the majority cooperation with CDU/CSU was not possible.

54 CDA together with VVD formed a coalition in the years 1977–1981 and 1982–1986, along with the party Pim Fortuyn (LPF) 2002 (first government of Jan Peter Balkenende), second government of Jan Peter Balkenende CDA, VVD with the Democrats 66 (D'66) in 2003. Subsequently, they ruled together until 2006 (third J. P. Balkenende minority government). Governmental cooperation continued between the parties with the support of the Party for Freedom (PVV) in the years 2010–2012 (the first Mark Rutte's government). The core of the third Mark Rutte's government after the last parliamentary elections in 2017 is composed of VVD, CDA, and D'66, CU (Christian Union).

ing coalition SDKÚ, KDH, SMK, and ANO from the years 2002–2006 (RILE index of 37.96), we would adhere to characterizing the first coalition government of Mikuláš Dzurinda as a minimum winning and ideologically connected, that is, homogeneous coalition. We have redefined the first government of Mikuláš Dzurinda SDK, SDĽ, SMK, and SOP (with programmatic differences of just 12.33 on the RILE scale) in line with the chosen approach as a wide and oversized, that is, constitutional and ideologically homogeneous coalition.

In the context of our hypothesis, which states that the emergence of antisystemic parties is related to vacating the extreme positions in the political spectrum, we can conclude that despite the increase of the ideological differences and variable tensions between the parties in the said period, the antisystemic KSS made it into Parliament. Its electoral success was associated in particular with the collapse of the established incumbent leftist parties and continuing division of the left, which resulted in the transfer of dissatisfied voters to a single leftist party. The empty space on the left in this period confirms the hypothesis that the emergence of antisystemic parties may be associated with vacating the extreme poles of the party system. The reason for this is the fact that although SMER presented itself as a socio-liberal project according to the model of the New Left, its program mostly matched the profile of a moderate centrist right-wing party with a preponderance of rightist topics and 8.86 on the RILE scale. This fact finally led the leftist voters, who were looking for leftist values, issues, and solutions, to ultimately choose KSS as the only clearly legible socialist party.

Early Parliamentary Elections in 2006

The participation rate in the 2006 early elections was at 54.67% of the eligible voters. In comparison with the year 1998 (84.24%) and 2002 (70.07%), we witnessed yet another decrease of 15.4% in voter turnout from the last parliamentary elections. In addition to the visible electoral slump of HZDS (lost of more than 358 thousand votes compared to the 2002 elections), SMER boosted its structures and electoral support thanks to the gradual integration of left-wing bodies.[55] Compared to 2002, SMER received 284,000

---

55 After the 2002 elections, SMER focused on the integration of non-parliamentary left-wing parties. At the beginning of 2003, it integrated SOP and in 2004 all other social-democratic

new votes. This factor caused SMER-SD to become a party with the highest number of electoral votes (671,185). The newly united SNS (after integrating Slota's PSNS)[56] made it into Parliament with almost 12% of the votes and 20 parliamentary seats. The presence of SNS in Parliament testifies to the nationalist cleavage in the Slovak party system. However, the socioeconomic cleavage and the urban-rural cleavage remained dominant in political competition. In terms of the number of seats and percentage of votes, the election results were as follows. SMER won 29.14% of the votes and 50 mandates, followed by SDKÚ-DS with 18.35% (422,815 votes) and 31 seats, SNS with 11.73% (270,230 votes) and 20 seats, SMK with 11.68% (269,111 votes) and 20 seats, ĽS-HZDS with 8.79% (202,540 votes) and 15 seats and KDH with 8.31% (191,443 votes) and 14 mandates.

The far-right parties Slovak People's Party with 0.16% (3815 votes), Slovak National Coalition - Slovak Mutuality with 0.17% (4016 votes), and also the liberal-centrist party Free Forum with 3.47% (79963 votes) of the departees from SDKÚ-DS and the former ruling party Alliance of a New Citizen with 1.42% (32775 votes) did not make it into Parliament. On the left side of the spectrum, the KSS with 3.88% (89 418 votes) or the former ruling party Union of the Workers of Slovakia in the years 1994–1998 with 0.29% (6 864 votes) were left out of Parliament.

After the early elections in 2006, the government was formed from the hitherto opposition or even non-parliamentary parties that profiled themselves against each other. Their cooperation, however, materialized when SMER-SD sent an offer to negotiate the government coalition to KDH. This party began to split on the basis of inter-party talks.[57] And although the potential cooperation of SMER and KDH would still require another partner, for example, SMK, it would not be sufficient for the SMER elites to secure a stable and dominant position in the government. There-

---

parties such as SDĽ, SDA, and SDSS. SMER added "Social Democracy" into its name and it completed the final transformation into a social-democratic party. This process resulted in SMER becoming a key leftist party in the Slovak party system.

56 The merger conference of both nationalist parties SNS and PSNS was held on May 31 in Žilina, with Ján Slota becoming its head and Anna Malíková its vice president. Subsequently, there were pending lawsuits to confirm the position of the legal representative between Anna Malíková and the fraction around Peter Sulovský, Viliam Oberhauser, and Jozef Prokeš. These were completed in 2004 by confirming Anna Malíková's position of a proper chairwoman and representative of SNS up until the merger conference. For more information, see Kopeček, 2007: 434–436).

57 The critics of the decision to initiate the government cooperation negotiations with KDH included the party's vice-presidents Daniel Lipšic, Vladimír Palko, Rudolf Bauer, František Mikloško, who first left the leadership and later the party itself.

fore, the leadership of SMER decided to offer cooperation to SNS and ĽS-HZDS.[58] SMER-SD, SNS, and ĽS-HZDS were intertwined by the same nationalist rhetoric, resistance to the reforms of the previous cabinets of M. Dzurinda, and the pragmatism in the context of political power. Since the end of the 1990s, these parties were continuously in opposition, or even outside of Parliament. Their leaders badly needed to succeed and ensure the survival and development of their parties. Despite the fact that it reached the worst electoral result under the direction of Vladimír Mečiar, the ĽS-HZDS could still grab a share of government power after two consecutive terms. The reason for this government was also the above polarization of the party system. This prevented a more intense programmatic consolidation and developed a fairly negative coalition potential (Klíma, 2001: 22) in the light of the personal animosities of its leaders. V. Mečiar's and J. Slota's non-participation in the government as leaders of government parties was SMER's condition for the governmental cooperation. This decision and its acceptance by ĽS-HZDS and the SNS were part of the calculation of acceptable political losses. The reason for this was the fact that the leaders of these parties were linked with alleged corruption cases during the third Mečiar's government.[59] For this reason, they as chairmen of their parties did not appear as nominees in the first government of Robert Fico but remained part of the unofficial government coordination platform in Fico's government, the so-called Coalition Council.

In comparison with the previous period, the government was formed on the principle of a minimum winning coalition of SMER-SD (50 seats), SNS (20 seats), and ĽS-HZDS (15 seats). At its inception, this government cherished the support of 85 mandates in the 150-seat Parliament. It is classified as ideologically connected in the literature on political science. Its formation was ultimately confirmed by the developments in the Slovak party system with polarized political parties as a result of the personal animosities of their leaders from the 1990s. Although the post-election rhetoric of the head of SMER-SD signaled the possibility of governmental cooperation with KDH, it eventually did not materialize. One of the reasons was also the dispute in SMER between the supporters and opponents of forming a government with KDH. The resulting 3-member coalition gov-

---

58 Real cooperation with SMK was impossible due to the nationalist rhetoric of SMER-SD and its leaders, which robbed the coalition parties ĽS-HZDS and SNS of their constituency.
59 For example, from the period of privatization of state property in the years 1994–1998 and serious political lapses, such as the kidnapping of Michal Kováč, jr., murder of Róbert Remiáš, revocation of František Gaulieder's MP mandate, disregard for the findings of the Constitutional Court of the Slovak Republic, etc.

ernment with Prime Minister Fico was a minimum winning coalition and it ruled for the entire term from July 4, 2006, to July 10, 2010. The problems related to maintaining this coalition as ideologically connected, however, were, for example, visible in the reaction of the Party of European Socialists (PES). PES suspended SMER's membership in its faction in the European Parliament after creating the government coalition with SNS. The SNS was viewed as nationalistic and extremely right-wing by its European partners, and its program was not in line with the social-democratic value system.[60] The unbalanced relationship in the government was also evident in SMER's over-representation in the executive branch with 11 ministerial posts compared to 3 occupied by SNS and 2 by ĽS-HZDS. The ratio between the proportion of seats and the number of ministerial posts in the coalition suggests that SNS and ĽS-HZDS acquired a much smaller presence in the executive branch than in the Parliament. With SNS, the proportion of coalition representatives in the Parliament and in the executive branch was 23.5:18.75 and with ĽS-HZDS, the proportion was 17.7:12.5 (Balík, Havlík, et al. 2011: 213).

Let us have a closer look at how the programmatic parameters of the 2006 parties changed on the right-to-left axis.

Table RILE index of the parliamentary parties in the 2006 elections

KDH	29.68
SNS	7.59
ĽS-HZDS	0.00
SDKÚ-DS	-1.25
SMK	-7.27
SMER-SD	-21.76
Variable range of the parliamentary parties and their programs	51.44
Turnout	54.67%
Programmatic differences in the SMER-SD, SNS, and ĽS-HZDS coalition	29.11

Source: Manifesto Project. Social Science Research Center Berlin [on line 25.4.2019]. Available on https://visuals.manifesto-project.wzb.eu/mpdb-shiny/cmp_dashboard_dataset/

---

60 The membership of SMER-SD in the PES was restored in 2008.

Chart: Ideological positioning of the parties in 2006 according to the RILE index

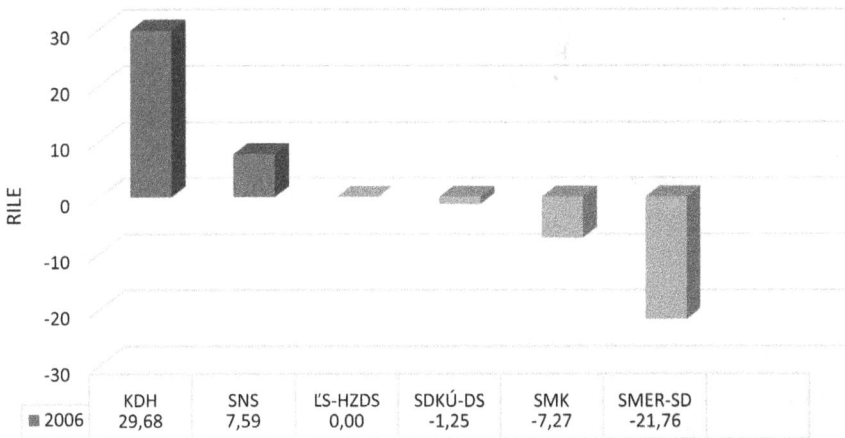

	KDH	SNS	ĽS-HZDS	SDKÚ-DS	SMK	SMER-SD
■ 2006	29,68	7,59	0,00	-1,25	-7,27	-21,76

The summary result of the RILE index, which is determined by the difference between the variable of rightist and leftist topics was as follows: SMER-SD confirmed its presentation as a leftist, social-democratic party with the result of -21.76. After the integration of smaller leftist democratic bodies since its inception (when it defined itself as a liberal left) with the RILE index of a centrist party of 8.86 in 2002), this party moved to the extreme left side of the party spectrum. This result therefore corresponds with its media presentation as a party to "fix" the numbingly implemented economic reforms of Dzurinda's governments. A similar result was also noted in the rightist KDH, whose result of 29.68 confirmed its presentation as a right-wing party (RILE index of 27.19 in 2002). KDH became a polar right-wing party in the party system, whereas SDKÚ-DS has significantly shifted to a centrist position. SDKÚ-DS shifted from its extreme position in 2002 (RILE index of 37.36) to the final leftist value of -1.25. This indicated a slight predominance of leftist topics and the transformation of SDKÚ-DS from a rightist party in 2002 to a centrist one. The reason for this was the emphasis on the socio-economic issues, which reflected the consolidation of the parties in the context of the socio-economic cleavage and urban-rural cleavage. The total variable range between these two extreme parties on the right-to-left scale of the political spectrum, however, grew yet again from 44.5 on the RILE scale in 2002 to 51.44 in 2006 even despite the fact that KSS did not make it into Parliament in 2006. This reduced the number of parties in Parliament, but it did not eventually lead to a reduction of ideological polarization of the party system. Quite the contrary.

Even this factor proves the preservation and augmentation of ideological distance between the relevant parties. Compared to the elections in 1994, the polar parties in the political spectrum once again moved further from each other. This is evidenced by the fact that the variable range was 14.72 in 1994, 21.04 in 1998, 44.5 in 2002 (if KSS were an irrelevant party, the RILE score of the variable tensions in the party system would be 37.36). These data confirm the deepening ideological polarization of the party system in Slovakia. The other parties filled the space between the polar parties of the ideological continuum, that is, between SMER-SD and KDH in 2006. The program of the traditionally nationalist party SNS turned out to be rightist with the index of 7.59, which maintained its rightist program and the resulting centrist orientation since 1998. ĽS-HZDS positioned itself exactly in the center of the political spectrum with 0.00 on the RILE scale, which also reflects its public presentation.

The programmatic positions of the ruling parties make us conclude that the ideological span between the parties of this coalition was 29.11 because ĽS-HZDS had a positional value of (0.00), the left-wing SMER-SD of (-21.76) and right-wing SNS of (7.35).

This value is higher than the value of the HZDS, SNS, and ZRS coalition after the 1994 elections where this difference between the government parties was 14.72 on the RILE scale. Paradoxically, the smaller distance between the parties in the government coalition was also present in the first Dzurinda's government (1998–2002), which had a value of 12.33 despite the fact that it was a wide and sizable coalition. By contrast, Dzurinda's second cabinet, which is often characterized as programmatically homogeneous, exhibited programmatic tensions of 37.36 on the RILE scale. By way of comparison, despite the fact that it was composed of SMER-SD, SNS, and HZDS, the first cabinet of Robert Fico exhibited a greater degree of programmatic homogeneity at 29.11 within the RILE index. Of course, given the SMER-SD's representation in the government and in Parliament, the government was characterized by the predominance of leftist topics and solutions.

Continuous parliamentary representation was maintained by KDH, SNS, ĽS-HZDS, and SMK. Based on the RILE index, even the SMK's program (-7.27) can be characterized as a leftist program. In the case of KDH, we see that since 1994 it has visibly shifted from the area of centrist-oriented left (-6.79 on the RILE scale) through the 2002 (27.19) and 2006 elections (29.68) into the dominance of right-wing topics in its program. The SNS had always kept the structure of a centrist and nationalist formation, although there is a visible shift from the dominance of left-wing themes in 1994 (-1.54) to the preponderance of right-wing topics in the 1998 election (13.86) and

2006 (7.59). Minimum program shifts were experienced in HZDS and SMK. The ĽS-HZDS only slightly shifted from its centrist position of a catch-all party in 1994 (RILE score at 2.66). In the year 1998, it scored 0.75 and in 2006 it had 0.00 on the RILE scale. The only and isolated reorientation in its program can be seen in 2002. In the parliamentary elections of 2002, its program shifted dramatically to the dominance of right-wing themes and solutions, and its value on the RILE scale totaled 20.63. The program of the SMK (whose original parties were partly represented by ESWMK in 1990, MKM-EGY in 1992, and MK in 1994) has since 1990 and 1992 moved from the centrist-right (5.26 in the RILE in 1990) to the centrist left in 1994 (RILE score of -5.69) with a slight predominance of left-wing themes. Since this period, SMK has oscillated only within the framework dominance of left-wing themes. Since 1998 from -7.18 to 2002 and the centrist position with -0.60 on the RILE index. Before the parliamentary elections in 2006, SMK returned almost to its original level from the second half of the 1990s, that is, -7.27 on the RILE scale. Even this fact suggests that the participation of SMK in Mikuláš Dzurinda's government was rather the result of an unusual cleavage mečiarism vs. antimečiarism, which was intensified by the nationalistic cleavage. In the opposite case, had the political parties cooperated on the basis of closeness of their political programs, the SMK with its voters mainly from the southern parts of Slovakia would have (according to RILE) would theoretically have a closer relationship with the centrist and leftist parties. The starting point of this statement is the fact that from 1994 the cooperation of ethnic hungarian parties (up to 2016) primarily focused on the development of cooperation of centrist and right-wing parties. This fact is also evidenced by the participation of SMK in two coalition governments of M. Dzurinda from 1998 to 2006.

If we perceive SDKÚ-DS as a successor of DÚ, we can conclude that despite the right-wing rhetoric of party, it has profiled itself as right-wing to centrist in the long term. In 1994, the DÚ RILE index reached 2.4. In 2002, SDKÚ had reached the value of 37.36 in the RILE index (which is nothing unusual in 2002 since most programs in this period reached the position of programs with a preponderance of right-wing topics). In 2006, it returned into the position of a centrist party as SDKÚ-DS with a slight predominance of leftist topics (-1.23). Even this shift indicates that in 2006 after the entry of the Slovak Republic into the EU structures, the focus of the programs and campaign themes included, in particular, the socio-economic disparities between the various regions of Slovakia. Up to one third of the program of each parliamentary party was devoted to improving the welfare and quality of life (with SMER-SD, this was 41.10% and 29.07% with the rightist KDH).

If we inspected more closely the comparison of programmatic themes in the election year of 2006, we would see that similarly to 1994, the themes in the area of welfare and quality of life prevailed. The scattering in the representation of this theme is not high, as no radical leftist party of the ZRS type (as was the case in 1994) made it into Parliament. Following KDH, the lowest share of this theme in the program is held by SMK at 28.46%. The biggest programmatic differences between the SMER-SD, ĽS-HZDS, and SNS coalition parties were in the field of social arrangement, where SMER-SD devoted 19.34% to this topic in its program and ĽS-HZDS and SNS only 5.60% and 7.41%. SMER-SD only devoted 3.96% to foreign relations in its program, ĽS-HZDS 10.18%, and SNS 14.45%. Most valence themes between the parliamentary parties and in the coalition can be found in the area of education, regional policy, infrastructure development, foreign relations, environment, unemployment, and business environment. We identified no typical positioning theme across all the parties in the political spectrum. Nevertheless, the conflicting themes and different solutions were presented in the field of taxation, progressive taxation, paid higher education, etc. In these topics, however, the ruling coalition parties have held similar positions. In addition to the above valence themes, the government parties reached a high level of agreement even in the area of culture (preservation and protection of cultural values, improved financing), minority policy, taxes, and agriculture.

It follows from the above that according to the analysis of the individual programs and despite the visible dividing line in the party system, which was based on V. Mečiar, the consolidation and standardization of the party system in Slovakia continued. In political practice, however, the party system maintained the format of extreme pluralism – of the polarized pluralism type – given the number of relevant parties in Parliament. The variable range between the two ends of the spectrum, that is, the rightist KDH in 2006 (RILE index of 29.68) and SMER-SD (21.76) has increased substantially when compared to the 1994 elections. After a constant growth of the variable range between the programs of individual parties in Parliament in the 1998 (21.04) and 2002 (44.5) elections, the RILE index value in 2006 reached a level of 51.44. At the time of the early elections of 1994, the variable range between the centrist and slightly rightist HZDS, which represented an extremely rightist party with an index of 2.66, and ZRS standing on the opposite side with a RILE index of -12.06, was only 14.72. The relatively low variable range after the elections in 1994 ultimately allowed the parties to create a stable minimum winning and (according to the RILE index) programmatically homogeneous coalition because one of the key positioning themes was the governmental cooperation with V. Mečiar as head of HZDS. The mečiarism vs. antimečiarism cleavage (political liberalism vs. authoritarianism) slowly subsided in the development of the party system and programmatic orientation of the parties from 1994 to 2006. Although its distorting presence persisted in the Slovak party system, it was increasingly replaced by the socio-economic cleavage and urban-rural cleavage. The new two-bloc cooperation in the Slovak party system from the mid-1990s, however, continued to be polarized together with the polarization of the political system. However, its existence was already supported by new parliamentary bodies. In 1998, it was mainly SOP and in 2002 ANO and SMER, whose mutual competition with established parties led to a continuous growth of the variable range between the parliamentary parties.

Despite the fact that the government's minimum winning coalition of SMER-SD, SNS, and ĽS-HZDS, with a moderate degree of programmatic differences at the level of (29.11), this coalition can be described as relatively homogeneous. Despite the internal disputes, which in part had to do with winning similarly oriented voters within their electorates, this government coalition ruled the entire term until the next regular election in 2010.

However, the division continued in the opposition, especially in the ranks of the opposition party SMK. After Pál Csáky was elected party president in 2007 and replaced Béla Bugár in this function, the party split into two. Some of its members left in 2009 and founded the new civic-rightist party Most-Híd in cooperation with the liberal-oriented Slovak political elites. The long chairman of SMK Béla Bugár became its leader. The party was pragmatically focused on civic awareness and multiethnic cooperation between the Slovaks and the Hungarian minority in Slovakia. The liberal party Freedom and Solidarity (SaS), headed by its chairman Richard Sulík, was founded before the 2009 elections. The rest of the party structures of the original Hungarian Coalition Party transformed into a new party – Party of the Hungarian Community/Magyar Közösség Pártja (SMK-MKP) – with a similar program.

Parliamentary Elections in 2010

The 2010 elections confirmed the existence of ideological polarization and tensions between the two blocks that formed in the Slovak party system.

The 2010 parliamentary elections were won by SMER-SD with 34.79% (880111 votes) and 62 seats, followed by SDKÚ-DS with 15.42% (390,042 votes) and 28 mandates, Freedom and Solidarity (SaS) with 12.14% (307,287 votes) and 22 seats, Christian Democratic Party with 8.52% (215755 votes) and 15 seats, Most-Híd with 8.12% (205,538 votes) and 14 seats, and SNS with 5.07% (128,490 votes) and 9 seats. The sheer number of corruption cases from the period of the first Fico's government, as well as the battle for similarly oriented voters between the two parties of the former Fico's government (SMER-SD, SNS, and ĽS-HZDS), have contributed to the poor result of the SNS and they were the beginning of the end of ĽS-HZDS in Parliament. ĽS-HZDS of Vladimír Mečiar did not exceed 5% electoral threshold. [61] The far left-wing parties Union of the Workers of Slovakia with 0.24% (6196 votes) and KSS with 0.83% (21 104 votes) did not make it into Parliament either. The ĽS NS with 1.33% (33 724 votes) was unsuccessful on the extreme right side of the spectrum.

However, compared to 2006, the number of parties in the Parliament did not change – six parties remained.

In terms of the highest number of votes, the elections were won by SMER-SD, however, it wasn't able to negotiate a government majority in Parliament without the former government allies. Eventually, the government with a low coalition potential was formed by the centrist right-wing parties around SDKÚ-DS its election leader Iveta Radičová. The public declaration of non-cooperation of SaS, KDH, and Most-Híd with SMER-SD reaffirms the binary polarization and two blocs in the party system. In the parliamentary absence of ĽS-HZDS, Robert Fico, head of SMER-SD, became a polarizing person in the context of the Slovak political system. This is because of his populist and conflict-oriented style of politics, as well as opposition to his exercise of power and lack of political responsibility for the corruption scandals during his first government in 2006–2010.

The centrist-right government alternative formed thanks to the continuing personal antagonism between the leaders of the former coalition

---

61 Statistical Office of the Slovak Republic. [on line 25.4.2019] Available on http://volby. statistics.sk/nrsr/nrsr2010/menu/indexv.jsp@lang=en.htm We need to emphasize that the cleavage of the Party of the Hungarian Coalition (SMK) meant that some of its original constituency supported the newly created political entity Most – Híd, which also emphasized the civic principle in addition to the nationalist one. The division of the Hungarian-speaking voters resulted in the fact that since 2010 SMK-MKP failed to exceed the 5% parliamentary threshold (in 2010 with 4.33% and 109 638 votes, in 2012 with 4.28% and 109 483 votes, in 2016 with 4.04% and 105 495 votes). Statistical Office of the Slovak Republic. [on line 25.4.2019] Available on http://volby.statistics.sk.

of SMER-SD, SNS and ĽS-HZDS and the other hitherto opposition parties. The new governing coalition was formed around Iveta Radičová, head of SDKÚ-DS, and SaS, KDH, and Most-Híd. She formed a minimum winning coalition with a tight majority of 79 seats in Parliament. The representation of the parties in government was proportional to their electoral mandates. SDKÚ-DS had five ministries, SaS four ministries, and KDH and Most-Híd three ministries each. The governing majority, however, has been hindered by the fact that the SaS parliamentary ballot also included four candidates of the civic movement Ordinary People, and the Most-Híd ballot included four MPs from a small right-wing Civic Conservative Party – OKS.[62] The government majority in parliament was in fact maintained by six parties. The candidates of the political body Ordinary People (OĽ), who appeared on the 147th, 148th, 149th, and 150th place on the SaS ballot, made it into Parliament thanks to the sufficient number of preferential votes. Therefore, the research of the development of variable tensions in Parliament also includes the Civic Conservative Party (OKS). Its representatives were on the Most-Híd ballot. Of the 14 original OKS candidates, four made it into Parliament. [63] The structure of Radičová's government and/or representation of the individual parties in it followed the percentage of the mandates only in the case of four parliamentary parties. [64] The emergence of Radičová's government could suggest the creation of a programmatically close coalition with programmatic overlap after the 2010 elections. However, these were formulated very vaguely in the mission statement. This shortcoming, coupled with the organizational inconsistency of the ruling parties and the lack of discipline of the MPs, subsequently gave rise to political tensions despite the fact that the governmental bodies presented themselves as rightist, civic, and liberal. Despite the expected programmatic homogeneity of the government, practical problems emerged in its

---

62 This was formed after the election of Ľudovít Kaník as chairman of the Democratic Party in May 2001. Consequently, most of the well-known conservative members of DS (J. Langoš, P. Zajac, F. Šebej, P. Tatár, P. Osuský and others) left the party and founded the OKS. It was a marginal political body, which after the failed elections in 2002 and 2006 managed to negotiate electoral cooperation with Most-Híd, which has allowed some of the representatives of OKS to appear on its ballots.

63 Peter Zajac from 13th place, Ondrej Dostál from 23th place, František Šebej from 33th place and Peter Osuský from 43th place in OKS. Before the 2012 election the original members of OKS appeared on the OĽaNO ballot, but after the disagreements with its leader Igor Matovič, they discontinued their cooperation with OĽaNO and withdrew from the ballot.

64 For the exact percentage of seats in Parliament and positions in the government, see (Balík, Havlík, et al. 2011: 213).

stability. Apart from personnel matters, these had to do with yet another standard cleavage in the party system. The already existing socio-economic and nationalist cleavage in the Slovak party system has been extended by another one: state–church. During the rule of this government, however, the party system showed an increasing presence of the European integration cleavage. This is related to the perception of transferring the sovereignty – from the nation State towards transnational institutions of the European Union. This cleavage happened to be on the axis of euroscepticism vs. europeanism. Its foundations started to shape in the Slovak party system before the entry of the Slovak Republic into the EU structures in the 2002–2006 election period.[65] To use the typology of Peter Kopecký and Case Mudde, the governing parties (SDKÚ-DS, KDH, and Most-Híd) manifested their attitudes in the dispute concerning the entry of the Slovak Republic into the European stability mechanism (ESM) in either approving of the attitudes of the so-called euroenthusiasm, or reservations of the so-called euroskepticism (SaS). In the first vote on the first provisional bailout fund (European Financial Stability Facility – EFSF) in May 2010, SaS supported it in Parliament. However, SaS rejected the subsequent creation of a permanent bailout fund, the so-called ESM, in October 2011. The European Stabilization Mechanism theme created space for a clearer differentiation between the positions of the political parties to the monetary and economic policy of the EU. In particular, the individual attitudes of the parties in the context of euroenthusiasm vs. euroscepticism were demonstrated against the proposed solutions of central political and economic institutions of the European Union. SaS has generally supported the European integration project, but rejected the said economic policy of the EU and the subsequent development in the context of the Eurozone and the Greek debt (Havlík, Kaniok, et al., 2006: 16).[66] The communications heterogeneity of the ruling coalition was augmented by the fact that Prime Minister Iveta Radičová did not have full control of the structures and her parliament group because she gave up on the opportunity to become head of SDKÚ-DS. Her efforts as a prime minister for a wider programmatic compromise were subsequently compromised by the disputes between the liberal SaS and the conservative KDH, for example, in the cultural and ethical issues. This was particularly revolving around the legalization of same-sex couples in

---

65 For more information, see Šedo, et al. 2003: 38–83).
66If we wanted to use different terminology, SaS assumed an attitude of the so-called soft Euroscepticism, and the other government parties defended the position of functional Europeanism.

registered partnerships or decriminalized of marijuana, separation of state and church, etc. All these factors later manifested themselves in the instability of parliamentary support for the various government proposals, coupled with the aftereffects of the financial crisis of 2008. The government efforts to consolidate public finances were implemented during the financial and economic crisis and rising unemployment. Despite the fact that all four coalition parties declared their adherence to rightist economic principles, their programs were contradictory on many counts. The most obvious differences were in the above cultural value orientation. These tensions intensified when the candidates of OĽ and OKS did not always support the government's opinions. This inconsistency was subsequently exhibited by lower work efficiency of the MPs, and the mutual distrust between the leaders of the ruling parties grew even further. This distrust was most obvious during the election of Attorney General. The coalition frictions, however, culminated in the context of the vote on the European Stabilization Mechanism. The declining public support for the governing parties was also noted by the SaS leaders as a reason for a more severe enforcement of its program. The polarizing coalition clash regarding the accession of the Slovak Republic to the ESM mechanism was joined by the prime minister with a vote of confidence.[67] The proposed law to ratify the ESM was not passed by the Parliament. Iveta Radičová's government thus had no confidence although the coalition parties SDKÚ-DS, KDH, and Most-Híd supported the entry of Slovakia into the ESM system. This was the first time in Slovakia since 1990 that the demise of a ruling coalition was declared on the basis of its own vote of confidence. This fact confirmed the establishment of yet another cleavage in the Slovak party system, but also insufficient stability of the government when the prime minister loses full control of the party structures, which he/she represents. The support or rejection of the expansion of political and economic processes within European integration became an integral part of the political battle from this point on between the parties in the party system.

Using the RILE scale, we can conclude that SMER-SD had the most leftist government program in the 2010 elections (-16.20). The other side of the party spectrum was occupied by the rightist OKS with a score of 34.73.

---

67 The essence of the said dispute consisted in the fact that the extraordinary summit of Heads of State and Governments of the Euro area in 2011 was attended by the prime minister without a mandate of the Committee for European Affairs. Thus, she participated in the international agreement for the provision of the second aid package to Greece without a prior mandate of the relevant parliamentary committee, the coalition agreement, or without a broader political consensus of the coalition and opposition parliamentary parties.

This party, however, did not appear independently in the elections. Its MPs, however, made it into Parliament on the Most-Híd (9.65) ballots and created a tight ruling majority (79 seats out of 150). For this reason, it is important to include them into the analysis of the evolution of the types of coalitions in this period. OĽ and OKS and their MPs must therefore be seen as an important part of the ruling majority in Parliament although as independent actors they were not originally part of the coalition agreement. SDKÚ-DS, the strongest government party, had a centrist program with a slight predominance of leftist themes at a level of - 3.54 on the RILE scale. With the predominance of rightist themes Bridge (9.65) has settled to the right of the center of the political spectrum, and some of its electorate and topics were taken over from the original SMK. In contrast, however, it moved programmatically to the right, which corresponded to its ideological profiling as a liberal and civic entity with an emphasis on regional development. Vladimír Mečiar's ĽS-HZDS did not make it into Parliament with its rightist-centrist program and a value of 12.02. Therefore, it is not listed among the relevant parties. SDKÚ-DS had a slight predominance of leftist topics compared to 2006 (-1.25), and it remained in the centrist-left position. In the year 2010, it slightly shifted to the left at the level of -3.54 on the RILE scale. Since 2006 when its program was at 29.68, KDH shifted more to the center with 14.15 on the RILE scale. On the contrary, SNS moved to the right from 7.59 in 2006 to 13.28 in 2010. The newly established liberal SaS completed the right side of the spectrum with a value of 30.28.

Table RILE index of the parliamentary parties in the 2010 elections

OKS	34.73
SaS	30.28
KDH	14.15
SNS	13.28
Bridge (Most-Híd)	9.65
SDKÚ-DS	-3.54
SMER-SD	-16.20
Variable range of the parliamentary parties and their programs	50.93
Variable range without OKS	46.48
Turnout	58.84%
Programmatic differences in the coalition SDKÚ-DS, KDH, Most-Híd	33.82
Programmatic differences in the coalition SDKÚ-DS, SaS, KDH, Most-Híd + OKS	38.27

Source: Manifesto Project. Social Science Research Center Berlin [on line 25.4.2019]. Available on https://visuals.manifesto-project.wzb.eu/mpdb-shiny/cmp_dashboard_dataset/

Chart: Ideological positioning of the parties in 2010 according to the RILE index

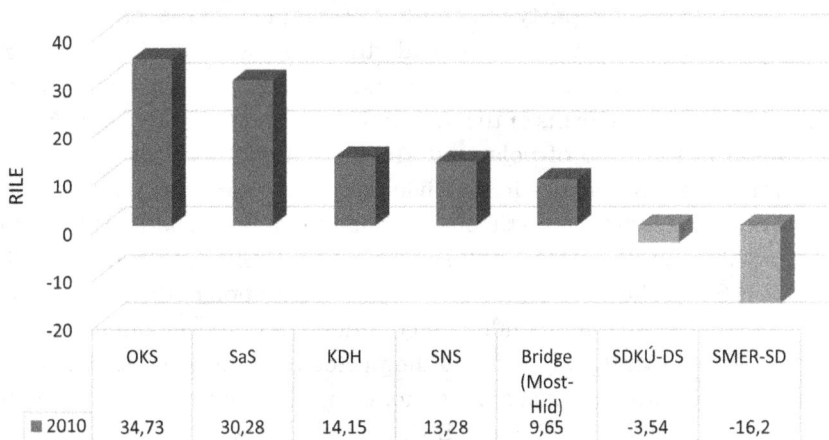

	OKS	SaS	KDH	SNS	Bridge (Most-Híd)	SDKÚ-DS	SMER-SD
2010	34,73	30,28	14,15	13,28	9,65	-3,54	-16,2

The variable range between the parliamentary parties in 2010 slightly diminished to a level of 50.93 when compared to 2006 (51.44).

If not for the OKS program, however, whose representatives made it into Parliament on the Most-Híd ballot, the variable tensions of the party system would be at 46.48. This figure, however, is not relevant since the members of the non-parliamentary OKS (and also OĽ) created the necessary governing majority in the Parliament. Even for this reason, their representatives without Peter Zajac and Igor Matovič were later incorporated into the coalition council. The programmatic span between the programs of the governing parties in 2010 increased compared to 2006. In 2006, the programmatic difference between the leftist SMER-SD (-21.76) and rightist SNS (7.35) was 29.11 on the RILE scale in the coalition of SMER-SD, SNS, ĽS-HZDS. In Iveta Radičová's government, and including OKS whose MPs helped to form the ruling majority of 79 votes, we arrive at 38.27 on the RILE scale. This difference is therefore wider than the difference in the first Robert Fico's government. When counting the official parties only, that is, those that signed the coalition agreement (SDKÚ-DS, SaS, KDH, and Most-Híd), the RILE score would be 33.82. This figure also reflects the nature of Radičová's coalition government – it was programmatically more heterogeneous than the one of R. Fico.

In general, and despite the minimum reduction of variable range of the parties in Parliament, we can observe a consolidation of the centrist leaning of the political parties and their programs. This trend is evident not only in the leftist SMER-SD, but also in the rightist SDKÚ-DS, KDH, and the newly emerged Most-Híd. SaS became a parliamentary party on the extreme right and it ousted KDH, which had occupied this position since 2006. No antisystemic party made it into Parliament in this period. All extremist parties have remained outside the framework of parliamentary politics. The party system, however, remained highly fragmented and extremely pluralist. In terms of the inter-party competition, the party system remained in the state of polarized and centrifugal political competition between the ruling parties in the civic-rightist bloc and the parties in the leftist-nationalist bloc. Apart from the nationalist SNS and ĽS-HZDS, this group of parties in this period also includes SMER-SD. Although the leader of SMER-SD declared the socio-democratic orientation of the party before the elections in 2012, in actuality he continued taking over the nationalist themes. He personified himself as the protector of national and state interests of Slovakia and was able to mobilize a significant part of constituency of the former ĽS-HZDS and SNS.[68] That fact was also reflected in the RILE index: when compared to 2006, SMER-SD moved from -21.76 to -16.20. It still, however, retained the position of a dominant leftist party. This was reflected in the persistence of centrifugal political competition and/or polarization even though the party that started it (ĽS-HZDS) did not make it into Parliament in 2010. SDKÚ-DS replaced it in the centrist position, and the variable tensions remained almost unchanged despite the shift of other parties to the center of the party system. In 2006, the variable range reached 51.44 on the RILE scale, and in 2010 it moved to a similar level of 50.93. This fact demonstrates the persistence of substantial ideological differences between the parties in Parliament. Similarly, the nature of political competition did not change, and the centrifugal tendencies prevailed over the centripetal. The intense conflict within the coalition and the opposition parties continued, and it constituted the prerequisites for a zero-sum game. In a situation where the MPs of the ruling coalition exhibited partisan intemperance, the political development resulted in a loss of confidence in Parliament and the subsequent early elections.

---

68 The nationalist rhetoric of SMER-SD was also demonstrated in the structure of the constituency between 2010 and 2012. The voters who voted for nationalist parties in 2010, for example, SNS and ĽS-HZDS, turned particularly to SMER-SD in the early elections of 2012. In the case of ĽS-HZDS voters, it was 47% in 2010 and in the case of SNS it was 20%. SMER-SD managed to reach 37% of the non-voters (in 2010) in the early parliamentary elections in 2012. For more information, see Verejná mienka a voličské správanie (Bútorová, Gyárfášová, Slosiarik, 2012). Public opinion and voting behavior [on line 25.4.2019]. Available on https://alianciazien.files.wordpress.com/2014/10/volby-2012-od-zb.pdf.

Early Parliamentary Elections in 2012

Major changes occurred in the Slovak party system after the early elections in 2012. Compared to 2010 (58.83%), the turnout slightly rose to 59.11% of all eligible voters. However, there were no substantial changes in the composition of the political representation in the Parliament in terms of the number of parties. The already established parliamentary parties such as SMER-SD, SDKÚ-DS, KDH, SaS, and Most-Híd were joined by the movement OĽaNO. The elections were won by SMER-SD with 44.42% (1,134,280 votes), which managed to form a uniform majority government (which is quite unusual in the Slovak political system) with 83 seats in the 150-seat parliament. Compared to the elections in 2010, SMER-SD grew by 21 seats. This result was unique in that it managed to produce a highly proportional electoral system in the Parliament. The Slovak electoral law, which was passed in 1998, stipulates the formation of one electoral district for the parliamentary elections, which creates the prerequisites for highly proportional election results irrespective of the applied method, but at the same time, it fosters the fragmentation of the party system. The resulting situation was partly due to the previous instability and discord of the right-ist-centrist government of Iveta Radičová, and the ability of SMER-SD to reach out to the voters of other parties of the former opposition (SNS, ĽS-HZDS) and the non-voters. Five more parties made it into Parliament. Chris-tian Democratic Movement with 8.82% (225,361 votes) and 16 seats, OĽaNO with 8.55% (218,537 votes) and 16 mandates, Most-Híd with 6.89% (176,088 votes) and 13 mandates, SDKÚ-DS with 6.09% (155,744 votes) and 11 seats, and Freedom and Solidarity with 5.88% (150,266 votes) and 11 mandates. In addition to SMER-SD, the number of seats in the Parliament increased by one for KDH and 12 for OĽaNO, a civic-conservative movement of Igor Matovič, this time as a standalone body. Other parties reported losses. The highest loss of 17 parliamentary seats was recorded by SDKÚ-DS, followed by SaS with 11 seats. It was due to the fact that the public viewed these par-ties as a cause of instability in the previous Radičová's cabinet. However, even the parties from Fico's first government (July 4, 2006–July 10, 2010) did not make it into Parliament. One of the factors that prevented SNS from exceeding the 5% threshold for entry into the Parliament was the de-parture of Anna Belousovová from SNS in 2011. She founded a new party called Nation and Justice – Our Party (NaS-NS), which, however, won only 0.63% (16 234 votes) in the 2012 elections. However, these votes were taken from SNS, which after winning only 4.55% (116,420 votes) – just like in 2002 after the split of the party structures and electorate – did not exceed the 5% threshold. A similar situation occurred in the case of ĽS-HZDS. This party won only 0.93% (23,772) of the votes and it did not get into Parliament for the first time since its inception. This result launched the marginalization of ĽS-HZDS into the position of an irrelevant political entity, which failed to transform into a programmatically targeted party. Since the history of HZDS was significantly marked by the personalization of the party with its leader Vladimír Mečiar, the same fate befell his party after the decline of his popularity due to the sheer number of corruption cases and the style of his leadership. This party did not overcome the developmental stage of a charismatic-crony party.

Of the extremist parties, the far leftist KSS with 072% (18,583 votes) and the right-wing ĽS NS with 1.58% (40,460 votes) did not exceed the parliamentary threshold.

All relevant parliamentary parties focused particularly on social care and welfare, and quality of life, economy, and political system are arranged in this order of appearance in four of the nine analyzed parties (SMER-SD, SDKÚ-DS, KDH, and Most-Híd). Exceptions to this order and emphasis can be seen in SAS and OĽaNO. When compared to 2010, the structure of election topics suggests that the most widely developed areas have remained the same for most of the parties, that is, no major programming changes in their programs have been implemented.

Based on the data from the preelection programs of the parties, we were able to place the investigated parties onto the RILE scale similarly to the analysis of party manifestos in the 2010 elections. After the early elections in 2012, the left part of the political spectrum is dominated by SMER-SD with a value of -9.73. On the contrary, the most rightist party was SaS with 25.66. The following table summarizes the measured values on the RILE scale:

Table RILE index of the parliamentary parties in the 2012 elections

SaS	25.66
OĽaNO	21.76
KDH	8.25
SDKÚ-DS	6.03
Bridge (Most-Híd)	-3.36
SMER-SD	-9.73

Variable range of the parliamentary parties and their programs	35.39
Turnout	59.11%
Programmatic differences in the coalition government	SMER-SD only

Source: Manifesto Project. Social Science Research Center Berlin [on line 25.4.2019]. Available on https://visuals.manifesto-project.wzb.eu/mpdb-shiny/cmp_dashboard_dataset/

Chart: Ideological positioning of the parties in 2012 according to the RILE index

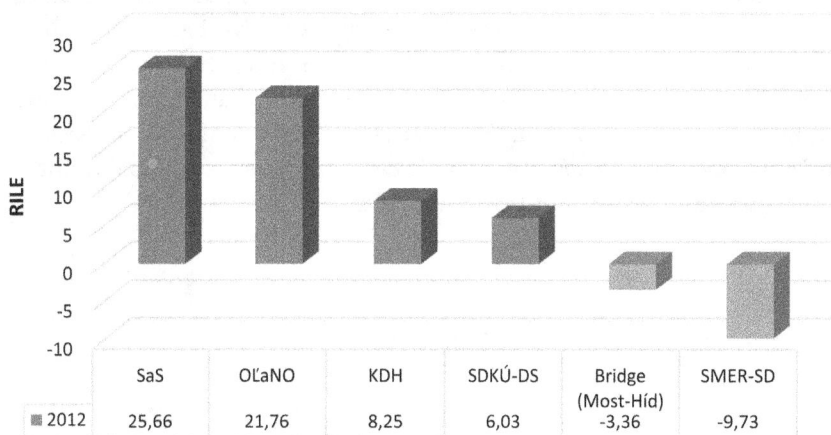

	SaS	OĽaNO	KDH	SDKÚ-DS	Bridge (Most-Híd)	SMER-SD
2012	25,66	21,76	8,25	6,03	-3,36	-9,73

Since following the elections of 2012, a uniform government under the leadership of SMER-SD was established, a paradoxical situation emerged in the Slovak party system. Despite the high degree of proportionality of the electoral system and fragmentation of the party system, the elections resulted in a single-party government headed by SMER-SD. This result is also interesting because the size and type of the party system has not changed and remained in the form of extreme pluralism, coupled with a high degree of polarization. Compared to the 2010 elections, the variable range between the leftist and rightist parties narrowed regardless of whether we take the 2010 RILE score of 46.48, that is, without OKS being part of the ruling coalition SDKÚ-DS, SaS, KDH, Most -Híd, or 50.93, that is, with OKS being part of the ruling coalition headed by I. Radičová, as a baseline. The parties mostly moved more to the center of the party spectrum (Most-Híd, SMER-SD, KDH, and SaS). A major change in the orientation of the party program can be seen in SDKÚ-DS, which has moved to the right of the spectrum from the original left-centrist position of -3.54 in the year 2010 to the level of 6.03 on the RILE scale. Similarly, OĽaNO filled the space on the right side of the spectrum between the liberal SaS and KDH. The party Freedom and Solidarity became a party on the extreme right of the political spectrum. The polarization of the party system remained unchanged despite the shift in most of the parties into the middle of the ideological continuum and a relatively high degree of concord in the valence issues. Let us mention just a few of these. There was a broad agreement on the need to tackle unemployment, new jobs, targeted promotion of employment of secondary school graduates, the unemployed 50 years and older, promotion of entrepreneurship, in particular small and medium-sized enterprises, reduction of the excessive length of state bureaucracy and judicial proceedings and their independence, growth of economic competitiveness, better transparency of public administration, e-government, subsidies from EU funds, etc. In view of the consolidation of the party system, the social-economic cleavage was stabilized, but the EU integration and urban-rural cleavage deepened.

Parliamentary Elections in 2016

After the regular parliamentary elections in 2016, the party system underwent some significant changes. Compared to 2012 (59.11%), the turnout increased slightly to a level of 59.82% of all eligible voters. In terms of the composition of political representation in the National Council of the Slovak Republic, the number of parties increased from six to eight. The incumbent parties such as SMER, SaS, Most-Híd, and OĽaNO were yet again joined by the SNS. What is more, two new parties made it into the Parliament. The centrist-right party Network (Sieť) of the former presidential candidate Radoslav Procházka, and the movement of the entrepreneur Boris Kollár with the name We Are Family – Boris Kollár (SME rodina – Boris Kollár).[69] However, the Parliament also opened its gates to the latently antisystemic extremist party K–ĽS NS of Marian Kotleba, a former

69 The movement We Are Family- Boris Kollár was founded in 2015 in opposition to the European immigration crisis. The founder of the movement Boris Kollár and his colleague M. Krajniak took advantage of the public discontent and concerns, which were caused by German Chancellor Angela Merkel and her open borders policy of October 2015. The movement cherishes conservative values on cultural and ethical issues, and its economic agenda can be characterized as centrist. The movement is not profiled ideologically and it is centrist oriented.

regional governor in the Banská Bystrica self-governing region.[70] For the first time since its inception, KDH did not make it into the Parliament with only of 4.94% (128,908) of the votes, and SDKU-DS with an election result of 0.26% (6938) of the votes. The radicalization of political discourse was notable particularly due to the public concern about uncontrolled migration, dissatisfaction with corruption, and increased ties between the parties and economic stakeholders. For example, these tendencies were also reflected in the switch of some of the voters of KDH, which until 2016 managed to integrate some sympathizers of the fascist people's regime (in the years 1939-1945).[71] These aspects were reflected in increased eurosceptic, isolationist, and nationalist sentiments in the general public. Although SMER-SD came out as the winning party from these elections, it received a much smaller number of votes compared to 2012. In 2016, this party fell to 28.28% (737,481 votes) and 49 seats in the Parliament. In terms of the votes, it was a drop by 396,799 voters. This drop in the number of votes was also reflected in the loss of mandates: SMER-SD lost 34 seats compared to 2012. Overall, its support fell back to the level in the 2006 elections. However, it remained the largest parliamentary party, and this advantage was also used in the negotiations to form the new government. The second highest number of votes was won by SaS at 12.10% (315,558 votes) and 21 seats, and the movement OĽaNO - NOVA strengthened its position to 11.02% (287,611 votes) and 19 parliamentary seats. These were followed by the nationalist SNS with a new leader Andrej Danko, electoral gain of 8.64% (225,386 votes) and 15 seats. Danko was elected Chairman of the SNS at the SNS Convention held on October 6, 2012, and he ousted J. Slota from this function. This change has resulted in the stabilization and increase of the membership base. Since 2012, the SNS membership has grown from 2335 to 7662 members in 2017. After 4 years, it yet again managed to regain representation

---

70 K-ĽS NS is an extremely right-wing party whose political representation is composed of the individuals who have repeatedly tried to get into the Parliament in the last parliamentary elections through right-wing extremist parties subscribing to the fascist Slovak state of 1939-1945 and glorifying Jozef Tiso and other representatives of this non-democratic regime.

71 This regime is characterized with the criteria presented by W. Merkel, who extended the Linz and Nolte typology of authoritarian regimes. The basic features of a fascist authoritarian regime include anticommunism, antiliberalism, the leadership principle, corporatist ideology, armed partisan militias and the corporative principle. For more information in this context, see Katuninec, M.: Režim slovenského štátu a jeho vývojové konotácie. In: Fiamová, M., Hlavinka, J., Schvarc, M., et al. Slovenský štát 1939-1945: predstavy a realita. Bratislava, Historický ústav SAV, 2014, 125-136. In the context of the complex relationship between the Church and the nation, see also Marchuk, 2016: 5-464.

in the Parliament.[72] The emergence of a far right extremist party K–ĽS NS with 8.04% (209 779 votes) and 14 seats was a fundamental novelty compared to 2012. This new parliamentary party was joined by another new movement We Are Family with a yield of 6.62% (172,860 votes) and 11 seats. The party Most-Híd slightly deteriorated its results compared to the 2012 elections from 6.89% (176 088 votes) to 6.50% (169,593 votes). It only received 11 seats, which meant a loss of 2 seats compared to 2012. The last party to have exceeded the 5% parliamentary threshold was the new centrist party Network with a gain of 5.60% (146,205 votes) and 10 seats. The ethnically oriented Party of the Hungarian Community – Magyar Közösség Pártja (SMK – MKP) with a yield of 4.04% (105,495 votes) and KSS with a gain of 0.62% (16,278 votes) did not make it into the Parliament. In addition to SaS, which gained 10 more seats compared to the 2012 elections, even the civil-conservative movement of Igor Matovič OĽaNO managed to increase its number of seats from 16 to 19.

The increased number of parties also meant an increase in the fragmentation of the party system. The ideological polarization of the party system also increased due to the program characteristics of the new parliamentary parties. The party system retained its extremely pluralist format. The post-election cooperation of SMER-SD and SNS, which was fueled by the acceptance of nationalistic themes by SMER-SD and an overlap in the socio-economic issues, was also maintained. Despite the biggest reduction in the number of mandates, SMER-SD remained dominant on the left.

However, fundamental changes occurred on the opposite side of the party system, as evidenced by the continued fragmentation of the right-wing spectrum. The parties that have long been considered relevant on the right side of the spectrum, such as KDH (128,908 votes and 4.94%) and SDKU-DS (6938 votes and 0.26%), remained outside the Parliament. In the case of KDH, this was a result of party management by Ján Figeľ. Figeľ was the KDH Chairman since 2009, but the party failed to integrate young people into the leadership and carry out the much-needed personal variation. After the 2012 elections, Daniel Lipšic and Jana Žitňanská left the party. In February 2013, the party lost Radoslav Procházka who failed to push through his modernization agenda titled Alpha. In March 2014, he took part in the presidential elections and won 21.1% (403,548) of the votes,

---

72 In the 2012 parliamentary elections, SNS only gained 4.55% (116,420 votes), which was not enough to cross the 5% parliamentary election clause. Subsequently, Andrej Danko was elected as the new party leader in October 2012.

which was enough for the third place. [73] R. Procházka used the potential and mobilized constituency from the presidential elections and established Network as a political party. The party was founded in June 2014 with the then MP for SDKÚ-DS Miroslav Beblavý, Andrej Hrnčiar, Mayor of Martin, Katarína Cséfalvayová and Katarína Macháčková, Mayor of Prievidza. The right-wing Network (Sieť) failed to materialize in the parliamentary elections despite the fact that it presented itself as an alternative to the leftist cabinet of SMER-SD. It only narrowly exceeded the 5% threshold, but thanks to its coalition potential it became a major player in search of the ruling parliamentary majority.

Due to the emergence of new right-wing parties such as SME rodina – Boris Kollár, but especially the extreme nationalist and xenophobic, conservative K-ĽS NS, the negotiations about the ruling majority were complicated. Network first attended an informal meeting with the leader of the right SaS about the formation of a rightist government. The post-election deadlock was finally resolved by the leader of Network R. Procházka and his decision to become part of the third government of Robert Fico together with Most-Híd. The party Most-Híd previously presented itself as a body criticizing the previous governments of R. Fico, and especially SMER-SD. The representatives of the centrist parties, such as Network (Sieť) and Most-Híd, preferred a coalition with SMER-SD and SNS compared to the larger alternative with SaS, OĽaNO, and We Are Family – Boris Kollár. In terms of the development of the hitherto inter-party cooperation, which was marked in the 1990s by the atypical transformation cleavage mečiarism vs. antimečiarism, the decision of the Most-Híd leadership to form a coalition with Robert Fico was striking to some members of the general public. The decision to form a ruling coalition with SMER-SD also meant a split, and later disappearance, of the Network (Sieť) parliamentary group. The reason was the disapproval of some of the MPs (M. Beblavý, K. Macháčková, S. Petrík) to join R. Fico's government. The disagreement later led to their departure from Network. This scenario, however, did not repeat in Most-Híd. An exception was the long-time member and Deputy Chairman of the party Zsolt Simon who left the Most-Híd parliamentary group. At the beginning of the term, the third cabinet of R. Fico relied on the mathematical support of 85 seats in the 150-seat Parliament. However,

---

[73] The then prime minister for SMER-SD Robert Fico and civic candidate Andrej Kiska made it into the second round of presidential elections. The latter won the second round with a yield of 59.4% (1,307,065) votes. The defeated candidate of SMER-SD Robert Fico won 40.6% (893,841) of the votes in the second round of presidential elections.

as we indicated earlier, after the formation of the government some of the MPs of the ruling parties Network and Bridge left the coalition majority and became independent.[74]

In late April, the 79 MPs of the coalition SMER-SD, SNS, Network, and Most-Híd approved the mission statement of the government and expressed support for the government in the Parliament. In practice, this resulted in the formation of a minimum winning coalition. However, together with the declining support for SMER-SD, the fragmentation of the party system required a larger number of coalition parties to form a majority than in 2012. In August 2016, R. Procházka stepped down as chairman of Network at the extraordinary congress of the party and the hitherto Minister of Transport Roman Brecely was elected a new party chairman. The break-up of the Network parliamentary group continued. Five MPs for this party joined the parliamentary group of Bridge. This resulted in a disappearance of the Network parliamentary group and it had an impact on the changes in the distribution of the various posts in the government and ministries. For this reason, September 1, 2016 a new coalition agreement was signed by the party chairmen of SMER-SD, SNS, and Most-Híd, resulting in the new minimum winning coalition government. This government divided 15 ministerial posts. The highest number of ministers (nine) was given to SMER-SD, SNS had three ministerial posts three and remaining three ministers were nominated by Most-Híd. For the third time, R. Fico became prime minister of the coalition government, which was in office from March 23, 2016, to March 22, 2018. In this government, SMER-SD occupied the following departments/ministries: Ministry of Finance of the Slovak Republic, Ministry of Foreign and European Affairs of the Slovak Republic, Ministry of Finance of the Slovak Republic, Ministry of Economy of the Slovak Republic, Ministry of Labor, Social Affairs and Family of the Slovak Republic, Ministry of Culture of the Slovak Republic, Ministry of Health of the Slovak Republic, and Deputy Prime Minister of the Slovak Republic for Investment and Informatization. The SNS won the following ministries: Ministry of Education, Science, Research and Sport of the Slovak Republic, Ministry of Defense of the Slovak Republic, and Ministry of Agriculture and Rural Development of the Slovak Republic. The liberal civic party Most-Híd won the Ministry of Environment, Ministry of Transport and Construction of the Slovak Republic, and Ministry of Justice of

---

74 Even some of the MPs for the movement We Are Family – Boris Kollár, namely Rastislav Holúbek, Martina Šimkovičová, and Peter Marček, left the parliamentary group of this party in June 2016.

the Slovak Republic. The distribution of positions in the executive branch was proportional to the parliamentary gain of the ruling parties.

The emergence of rightist parties – the extremist K–ĽS NS – in the Parliament was a fundamental novelty in comparison with the previous period. Its entry into the Parliament caused an increased ideological polarization even in the opposition ranks. Its emergence in the Parliament indirectly affected the formation of the government. From the perspective of political science, this party is a latent antisystemic entity, and it meets the attributes of ideological and relational antisystemicity (Kubát, 2010: 85). The far-right party K–ĽS NS is headed by Marián Kotleba who eventually succeeded at the national level as a party leader after several electoral failures with other political projects. In the first decade after 2000, Kotleba and his closest associates tried to establish themselves through Slovak Congregation (Slovenská pospolitosť), an organization initially registered as a civic association. After this civic association transformed into a political party – Slovak Congregation – National Party (SP-NS) – it was banned by the Supreme Court of the Slovak Republic on the initiative of the Prosecutor General in March 2006. The reason was the program objectives of SP-NS, which were in conflict with the Constitution (Kupka, Laryš, Smolík, 2009: 54). The ĽS NS program was a sophisticated rework of the program of the banned SP-NS in 2006. The program, however, lacked the idea of the corporative state, which has been identified as violating the Constitution. Subsequently, the collaborators of M. Kotleba joined the registered party Friends of Wine Party (Strana priateľov vína) in 2010. This party was taken over from the inside and it was renamed to People's Party Our Slovakia. Since November 2015, the party bears the name Kotleba – People's Party Our Slovakia. The leading representatives of this party regularly participated in the parliamentary elections. In the 2010 parliamentary elections, ĽS-NS won 1.33% (33,724 votes) and in the early parliamentary elections in 2012, it gained 1.58% (40,460 votes). It did not exceed the 5% threshold necessary for entry into the Parliament. A change occurred after the regional elections in 2013 when the party leader Marian Kotleba won the electoral battle for the presidency of the Banská Bystrica Self-Governing Region as an independent candidate (NEKA). The entry of ĽS NS into parliamentary politics in 2016 was preceded by the election of the party's chairman Marian Kotleba in the regional elections as Governor of Banská Bystrica Self-Governing Region . In the regional elections to the regional bodies (at that time, it was based on a two-round absolute majority electoral system), he made it to the second round. In it, after the undiplomatic public statements of the then Prime Minister Robert Fico but also some representatives of the rightist parties about M. Kotleba, the partisan influence was not used as a guide for the voters. For example, this is used by the pro-democracy parties in the French partisan politics between the first and second round of elections to marginalize extremist candidates. Because of the failure of the political elites from the incumbent parties and the ability of M. Kotleba to mobilize the disgruntled voters as an independent against the then candidate of the ruling party SMER-SD, he managed to win the protest votes. In the second round, M. Kotleba received 71,397 votes and defeated the candidate of SMER-SD – the then Governor of Banská Bystrica Self-Governing Region and MEP Vladimír Maňka. He only received 57,164 votes despite the fact that he had the support of SMER-SD, ĽS-HZDS, and HZD and KDH, SMK-MKP, SZ, and SMS in the second round. This was caused by a number of factors, ranging from the public disagreement with the decisions of the former government party SMER-SD with its governance, through the popularity of independent candidates in the elections to local governments, to the inability of the parliamentary parties across the political spectrum to agree on supporting a pro-democracy candidate. It is a fine example of how partisan polarization, low credibility of the parties, decline in the efficiency of public institutions and the rise of corruption affects the deepening mistrust of the citizens to the political parties. The dissatisfaction with the functioning of the political system is also reflected in the decrease of credibility of the liberal democratic institutions[75] and a parallel increase in the risk of public support for extremist groups. When we look at how these factors in the national policy led to the election of an independent with a proven antidemocratic mindset, we can conclude that it was the very decisions of the representatives of established political parties in the Parliament that mobilized the disgruntled voters. The accumulation of dissatisfied and politically undecided voters, the growing trend of aggregate volatility in the parliamentary elections since 2010–2012 (at a level of 26%) increased to 34.4% in the period from 2012 to 2016[76]. From this amount, altogether 11% represented the non-systemic level. In this group of voters, the decisions of the first-time voters are of a particular interest. In 2016, 22.70% of these voters voted for the extremist K–ĽS NS headed by M. Kotleba. Based on this support, it became a relevant parliamentary party in 2016. However, at the level of regional self-government, Kotleba did not

---

75 Gyárfášová, O. (2015): To sladké slovo demokracia ...Spokojnosť s demokraciou a politické odcudzenie na Slovensku. Sociológia, Vol. 47, No. 4, pp. 365-389. ISSN 0049 – 1225.
76 Gyárfášová, O., Slosiarik, M. (2016): Voľby do NR SR 2016: Čo charakterizovalo voličov. Working Papers in Sociology 1 [on line 5.5.2019]. Available on http://www.sociologia.sav.sk/pdf/Working_Papers_in_Sociology_012016.pdf.

make it as Governor of the Banská Bystrica Self-Governing Region in 2017. This loss was significantly aided by the decision of most of the pro-democratic candidates to step down from the race in favor of an independent candidate Ján Lunter. He had the highest preferences in the polls, which allowed him to create effective pressure even on the prodemocratic candidates. Before the elections to the regional bodies, the government had to modify the electoral system from an absolute majority system to a one-round relative majority system. Despite the increase in membership (ĽS NS or K-ĽS NS membership has risen since 2010 from 11 registered members to 1439 in 2017), the candidates for K-ĽS- NS did not make it in the 2017 regional elections. [77]

From the radical parties, the parliamentary threshold was not even exceeded by the far-leftist KSS with a gain of 0.62% (16 278 votes) whose support decreased slightly (0.72%, i.e., 18,583 votes) compared to the 2012 elections.

Most parliamentary parties focused mainly on national sovereignty in their programs, which has become an important issue in view of the ongoing wave of migration, social care, welfare and quality of life, economy, relations with the European Union, and corruption. Based on the data collected from the preelection programs of the political parties, we can place the analyzed parties on the RILE scale. After the regular parliamentary elections in 2016, the left side of the political spectrum was again dominated by SMER-SD. Its program had a value of -16.53 on the RILE scale, which means a shift to the left from a value of -9.73 on the RILE scale in 2012. SaS with a result of 28.38 on the RILE scale took the rightmost position in the party system even after the entry of the extremist K-ĽS NS into the Parliament. Compared to 2012 (25.66), this represents a slight shift of this party to the right. This information is important because the entry of the extremist and latently antisystemic party K-ĽS NS was not caused by emptying the right side of the political spectrum, as was the case in 2002. In this election year, the entry of KSS into the Parliament was caused by the shift in the political program of SMER to the moderate right (8.86 on the RILE scale) and by emptying the left side of the party system. The entry of the extremist K-ĽS NS into the Parliament in 2016 was caused by other factors. The most important ones include the loss of confidence in the es-

---

77 K-ĽS-NS won one MP place in the Banská Bystrica Self-Governing Region (Marian Kotleba – Chairman of LS-NS) and one in Nitra Self-Governing Region (Milan Uhrík – Vice Chairman of ĽS-NS) in the 2017 regional elections.

tablished parliamentary parties, [78]fear of migration, persistent regional socio-economic disparities,[79] corruption, and links between the political elites and economic interest groups. The following table summarizes the measured values on the RILE scale:

Table RILE index of the parliamentary parties in the 2016 elections

SaS	28.38
SNS	12.95
K-ĽS NS	8.99
We Are Family – Boris Kollár	2.11
Network (Sieť)	0.86
Most-Híd (Bridge)	0.44
OĽaNO	-2.43
SMER-SD	-16.53
Variable range of the parliamentary parties and their programs	44.91
Turnout	59.82 %
Programmatic range of the coalition	29.48

Source: Manifesto Project. Social Science Research Center Berlin [on line 25.4.2019]. Available on https://visuals.manifesto-project.wzb.eu/mpdb-shiny/cmp_dashboard_dataset/

Thus, the outcome of the parliamentary elections did not change the size and type of the party system. This remained in the form of extreme pluralism, and in combination with a high degree of polarization. As noted earlier, there was an increase in the programmatic differences at the extreme poles of the political continuum, both in the case of SMER-SD and SaS. Compared to the 2012 elections, the variation range of the programs of tye parliamentary parties slightly widened from a level of 35.39 to 44.91 on the RILE scale. This is also confirmed by the increased polarization of

78 This situation was identified in the analysis of the V4 countries, which confirmed that the Slovak population feels the highest mistrust in the political parties and institutions of representative democracy among the countries of Central Europe. Bútorová, Z., Mesežnikov, G., et al. *Aktívne občianstvo a občianska participácia na Slovensku a v krajinách V4* [on line 10.3.2019]. Available on http://www.ivo.sk/buxus/docs//rozne/Prezentacia_IVO_19_12_Aktivne_obcianstvo.pdf.
79 For more information on the regional factors that influenced the election of M. Kotleba as Chairman of the Banská Bystrica Self-Governing Region, see Buček., Plešivčák, 2017: 599–635).

Chart: Ideological positioning of the parties in 2016 according to the RILE index

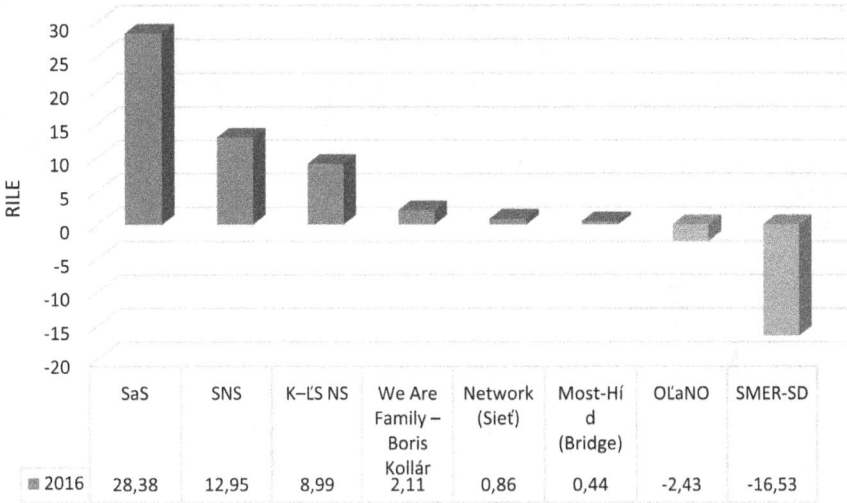

	SaS	SNS	K–ĽS NS	We Are Family – Boris Kollár	Network (Sieť)	Most-Híd (Bridge)	OĽaNO	SMER-SD
■ 2016	28,38	12,95	8,99	2,11	0,86	0,44	-2,43	-16,53

the party system, and again, at a relatively high agreement in the valency issues. In terms of consolidation of the party system, the socioeconomic cleavage was stabilized, and the euroenthusiasm vs. euroscepticism and urban-rural cleavage was accentuated. Despite intensive campaigning of the political parties, which was based on the distancing from the decisions and practices of the former ruling party SMER-SD, no atypical cleavage similar to mečiarism vs. antimečiarism was formed in the Slovak party system. In the context of the ruling coalition, the extreme positions were occupied by SMER-SD on the left and SNS on the right. The programmatic range of the coalition SMER-SD, SNS, Most-Híd, Network (Sieť), and later the coalition SMER-SD, SNS, Most-Híd remained unchanged at 29.48 on the RILE scale. Compared to the other coalition government, this figure stands at a level of the first government of Robert Fico (SMER-SD, ĽS-HZDS, and SNS 2006–2010 with 29.11 on the RILE scale). This figure also indicates that in terms of the programmatic homogeneity/heterogeneity of the ruling coalition on the RILE scale, the third Fico's government exhibits a higher programmatic agreement than, for example, Radičová's government (SD-KÚ-DS, SaS, KDH, and Most-Híd; 2010–2012; 33.82 on the RILE scale) and the second government of Mikuláš Dzurinda (SDKÚ, SMK, KDH, ANO; 2002–2006, 37.96 on the RILE scale).

The third cabinet of R. Fico with SMER-SD, SNS, Most-Híd, and Network (Sieť) can therefore be labeled as an ideologically connected minimum winning coalition. The most significant changes in the programmatic orientation of the parties can be seen in the movement OĽaNO, which transformed from a position of a right-wing party in 2012 (21.76 on the RILE scale) to a centrist party with a slight predominance of leftist themes (-2.43 on the RILE scale). Compared to 2012 when the party did not make it into the Parliament, the program of SNS changed only slightly toward the center from 15.42 to 12.95 on the RILE scale. The party Most-Híd has maintained its centrist position. It moved from the position of a centrist and moderately leftist party in 2012 (-3.36 on the RILE scale) to a centrist right position with 0.44 on the RILE scale.

The stability of government was shaken at the end of February 2018 by the murder of investigative journalist Ján Kuciak and his fiancée Martina Kušnírová. His work exposed the corrupt links between the leading representatives of the ruling party SMER-SD, the police, prosecutors, and the Slovak oligarchs. This event marked the emergence of the civil initiative Za slušné Slovensko (For decent Slovakia). The public protests organized by this initiative, the largest since November 1989, and the information on the links between the businessmen with ties to the Italian Mafia and the nominees of SMER-SD in the government, the police, and prosecutors, led to the withdrawal of the Minister of Culture M. Maďarič and Minister of Interior R. Kaliňák. The unrelenting public pressure subsequently led to the resignation of Prime Minister Robert Fico. As a leader of the strongest ruling party, he returned to the Parliament as an MP. After the changes in some ministerial posts, the ruling coalition continued in the same format under the leadership of the then deputy prime Minister for Investments Peter Pellegrini. On March 22, President A. Kiska appointed P. Pellegrini as prime minister after having received 79 signatures of the Members of Parliament. After the appointment, Pellegrini maintained his position as Vice-Chairman of SMER-SD.

Conclusion

In the present work, we tried to shed some light on the development of the Slovak party system after the political transformation from the communist regime in the period from November 1989 to the 2016 parliamentary elections. We tried to show how the individual parties within the framework of the political system correspond with their ideological and programmatic orientation. In the initial division of the parties, we followed the model of the party families introduced by Klaus von Beyme, which was supplemented by the RILE index and evaluations and opinions of the authors who dealt with the development of the political parties, party system, and the formation of government coalitions in Slovakia. We used the data from the international research CMP for the initial characterization of the programmatic orientation of the parties. In parallel, we tried to figure out whether the declared ideological orientation of the leaders and representation of the parties is in line with their program. Specifically, in determining the positional value of each political party, we used the RILE index as comprehensive image of the party's program. Since the ideological orientation of the parties and the diversity of their programs is still an important analytical tool based on the right-to-left orientation of the parties (the RILE index), we subsequently tried to characterize the degree of homogeneity and heterogeneity of the ruling coalitions using the same index. Our analysis of development of the Slovak party system also included the verification of a hypothesis, which states that the reduction of programmatic differences (ideological) of the parliamentary parties (on the RILE scale) and their routing into the center of the political continuum creates space for the promotion of antipolitical, antiestablishment and antisystemic or radical parties in the system of political parties.

As we have indicated in the introduction to our work, the positions of the parties on the right-left scale based on the RILE index values may not be in conformity with the positioning of the said parties on the right or left in the Slovak media and academic discourse. At the same time, the index of each policy area may be in the tension or contradiction to the resulting policy of the parties, for example, within the framework of the government. For example, in terms of its program, SMER-SD tends to be largely viewed as a leftist, social-democratic party; however, its presentation also includes nationalist rhetoric or decisions that are contrary to the objectives of standard social-democratic parties (such as the rights of the minorities, churches, etc.). HZDS was largely regarded as a centrist party but, due to its nationalist-populist character and authoritarianism of its leader V. Mečiar, it was a hardly identifiable political party. On the other hand, KDH tends to be described as a conservative, christian democratic party in most analytical works, SDKÚ-DS as a christian-liberal party, and MOS, MKDH, ESWMK, MKM-EG, MK, SMK, SMK-MKP as regional and ethnic parties. Most-Híd and the liberal SaS are quite often classed as liberal, or centrist-right parties. Compared to them, for example, the SNS is often ranked as extreme right and nationalist, and the Communist Party as extreme left. Such a distortion of the generally applicable categories on these groups of parties could be caused by highlighting just a single programmatic area, for example, economic priorities, which differentiate the parties by the method and width of state interventions into the economy, ideas about the specific model of the welfare state, or general rhetoric of the leaders. The CMP methodology and the RILE index, however, takes into account the wider context of the programming orientation of the parties. This quantifiable figure is based on the very programming documents, which are published by the parties before the parliamentary elections. For this reason, it is understandable that this comprehensive approach may change the overall perception and position of the parties within the framework of the left-right political continuum. However, as highlighted at the beginning of our work, the RILE index data do not always correspond to the specific party politics or its ideological self-identification. This is limited by a number of other external and internal factors, ranging from the international position of the country, its economic situation, through the polarization between the parties, to the intra-party relations.

A number of consolidation development tendencies can be observed in the development of the Slovak party system based on the data and the RILE scale. These will be characterized also in the context of the observed criteria of variable tensions in the party system and the programmatic homogeneity of the ruling coalitions.

The variable tensions between the extreme parties in the party system gradually subsided in 1990–1994. In this period, the development of the programmatic differences of the ruling coalition had a cosine trajectory. During the observed transition period in 1990–1994, the decreasing variable tensions of the party system were accompanied by decreasing programmatic differences of the ruling coalition only in 1990–1992. Despite the fact that from 1990 to 1994 the programmatic differences between the parties narrowed, no antisystemic or extremist party made it through the parliamentary elections.

The situation in 1994 was unique because the variable tensions (expressing the programmatic differences of the parliamentary parties) were equal to the programmatic differences of the coalition (14.72). The government was composed of parties from different political poles (HZDS, ZRS). However, these low programmatic differences of the ruling and parliamentary parties did not reflect the gradual increase in political polarization of the party system. The reason was mainly the ethnic cleavage, urban-rural cleavage, and mečiarism vs. antimečiarism cleavage.

In the context of increasing polarization between the parties established in the transition period (HZDS, SNS vs. KDH, DÚ, DS, SMK, SDĽ,
SDSS, SZS), we have noted a continuous growth of the variable range in
the party system from 1998 to 2006 when it reached a maximum value of
51.44 in the observed period. With insignificant fluctuations, the variable
range of the parties in the party system was also maintained in 2010. The
variable tensions in the RILE index had a value of 50.93 at that time. In the
period 1998-2002, the programmatic differences of the ruling coalition on
the RILE scale grew in synchrony with the rise of the programmatic differences between the parliamentary parties. The rise of the ideological range
of the parties in Parliament, however, did not always correspond with the
growth of programmatic differences of the parties in the ruling coalitions
(e.g., 2006, 2010, 2012, and 2016).

In terms of ideological homogeneity of the ruling coalitions, it is note-
worthy that the first ruling coalition of Mikuláš Dzurinda, which was in
power in the period 1998-2002 and which tends to be described as a broad
coalition because of the participation of SDK, SDĽ, SMK, and SOP in the
government, does not show high values of programmatic heterogeneity.
According to the RILE index, the programmatic differences in the first
Dzurinda's government were smaller than in the second Dzurinda's cabinet (2002-2006) and in the third Vladimír Mečiar's government (1994-1998).
Its programmatic dispersion is smaller even compared to all ruling coalitions after 2002 up until 2010, and are usually referred to as programmatically homogeneous. If we would like to maintain the validity of the
existing analytical reviews on the homogeneity/heterogeneity of the ruling
coalitions in the Slovak parliamentary system since 1990, it is necessary
to modify the characteristics of this coalition. In terms of the observed
programmatic deviations, the first Dzurinda's ruling coalition government (1998-2002) should be seen as a constitutional and programmatically
homogeneous coalition based on its programmatic differences (RILE index). We can observe an increase in the intensity of programmatic heterogeneity of the governments since 1998. The programmatic differences of the ruling coalitions reached the peak value in 2002 in the second
Dzurinda's government. In 2006, we noted a small decrease in the ideological differences between the ruling parties in R. Fico's first government,
which is in turn substituted by increased heterogeneity of the ruling coalition in Radičová's 2010-2012 government. It is also interesting to note
that the government of Iveta Radičová (2010-2012) could be considered the
most diverse government coalition since 1990 if we reckoned the members
of OKS who made it into Parliament on the Most-Híd ballot as an integral

part of the coalition. With the members of OKS as an official part of the coalition, Radičová's government would have had its programmatic differences at a level of 38.27. Without the members of OKS, its heterogeneity would lower to 33.82, but it would still be higher than in R. Fico's first government. The political analysts, however, view it as centrist-rightist. Third coalition government of Robert Fico and P. Pellegrini SMER-SD, SNS, and Most-Híd (from March 2016) had a similar position on the RILE scale (29.48) as the first Fico's cabinet (29.11), which was composed of SMER, SNS, and HZDS (2006–2010). These findings make us conclude that there is an indirect correlation between the development of the variable range of the parties in the Slovak party system and the programmatic closeness of the coalition governments. The reason for this conclusion is the fact that only in the period between 1990 and 1992, 1998 and 2002, 2010 and 2012, and 2012 – 2016, synchronization of development of monitored parameters can be observed. In the first case, it is a decrease in both analyzed criteria. In the years 1990–1992, the programmatic differences of the ruling coalition decreased along with the variable range of the political programs. In the second case, in the years 1998–2002 we can observe a synchronous rise of both variable and programmatic differences of the ruling parties. And in the years 2010–2012, we are again witnessing a synchronous decline of both monitored parameters. In the 2012–2016 term, one can note a synchronous rise of both the variable range in the programs of the parliamentary parties and the coalition program because in the 2012–2016 period, SMER-SD was the only government party.

The below data allow us to draw the following conclusions on the programmatic closeness of the ruling parties in the individual government periods.

Chart - Development of variable range of the parliamentary parties within the context of development of the programmatic differences on the RILE scale

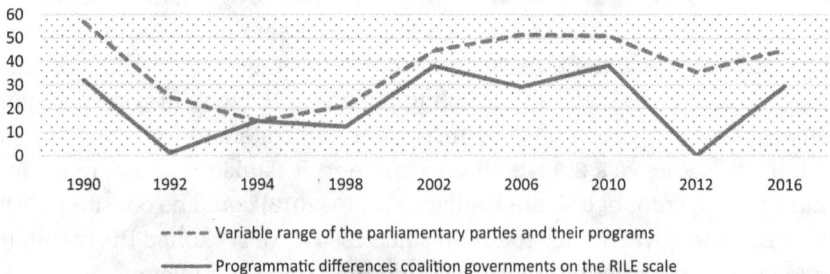

- - - - Variable range of the parliamentary parties and their programs

——— Programmatic differences coalition governments on the RILE scale

According to the RILE index, the most programmatically homogeneous coalition was the minimum winning coalition HZDS and SNS in the years 1992–1994. Until November 1993, the government and the HZDS cabinet were informally supported by SNS. After a schism in HZDS, the president nominated a new government, which was officially a coalition government and it consisted of ministers for HZDS and SNS. The programmatic differences of the ruling parties reached 1.06 on the RILE scale in this period. This period is followed by the first constitutional, that is, a broad, coalition of M. Dzurinda SDK, SDĽ, SMK, and SOP in the years 1998–2002 (12.33). The third programmatically homogeneous ruling group was the minimum winning coalition of Mečiar's third cabinet, which consisted of HZDS, SNS, and ZRS (14.72). The imaginary center of the analyzed ruling coalitions belongs to the coalition KDH, SDĽ, and ADS, which, however, was not formed after the elections but following the withdrawal of V. Mečiar's second government in March 1994. It was a minority government with the support of MKM-EGY. Its programmatic differences were at a level of 24.93 on the RILE scale, and it was terminated by the early elections, particularly due to the requirement of the then coalition socialist SDĽ.

We begin the overview of the heterogeneous ruling coalitions with the third coalition of R. Fico, which was formed after the 2016 elections. The government majority was formed by SMER-SD, SNS, Most-Híd and Network (after the collapse of the newly formed parliamentary coalition party Network, the coalition has stabilized in the form of cooperation between SMER, SNS, and Bridge). The programmatic differences in Robert Fico's (and later P. Pellegrini's) third government were at 29.48 on the RILE scale. This difference is also present in Fico's first cabinet and the triple coalition SMER-SD, SNS, and HZDS of the years 2006–2010. The ruling majority was created by SMER-SD, SNS, and ĽS-HZDS. The programmatic differences in Robert Fico's first government were at 29.11 on the RILE scale. It is followed by the ideologically connected ruling coalition of the parties from 1990. The parties VPN, KDH, and DS created a coalition government whose index of the programmatic differences was 32.05 on the RILE scale. According to the programs, M. Dzurinda's second coalition in the years 2002–2006 was the most heterogeneous ruling coalition government (SDKÚ, SMK, KDH, and ANO). The programmatic differences of these ruling parties were 37.96 on the RILE scale. The second most heterogeneous coalition government based on the RILE index (or at least programmatically close) was I. Radičová's government in the period 2010–2012. It was established after the elections on the basis of cooperation between the parties SDKÚ-DS, KDH, and Most-Híd with an index of 33.82 on the RILE scale. However, if we count in the members of OKS who got into Parliament on the Most-Híd ballot as part of the coalition and helped create the post-election ruling majority in Radičová's government and parliament, then this coalition aspires to occupy the post of the programmatically widest coalition in the monitored period until 2012. The reason for this is the fact that by adding the OKS program to the ruling coalition, the programmatic differences of Iveta Radičová's cabinet would increase to 38.28 on the RILE scale. However, if this party is not counted as member of the winning coalition (which was, however, formed with the necessary support of the OKS members), the index of the programmatic differences of the ruling parties would be 33.82, and it would be the second most heterogeneous ruling coalition. The position of programmatically most heterogeneous government would subsequently be occupied by Mikuláš Dzurinda's second government from the period 2002–2006 (programmatic differences of 37.96). If we remember that both above ruling coalitions, that is, Mikuláš Dzurinda's second cabinet and Iveta Radičová's government, ended their term with early elections, we can consider the programmatic heterogeneity – along with other indicators (connections between the party and government posts, partisan discipline of the ruling MPs, the manner in which the government plans were implemented, corruption cases, method of communication of policies, etc.) – to be an important indicator, which has an impact on the stability of government in the Slovak parliamentarism.

Chart: The development of variable range between the parliamentary parties and programmatic differences in the 1990–2016 coalition.

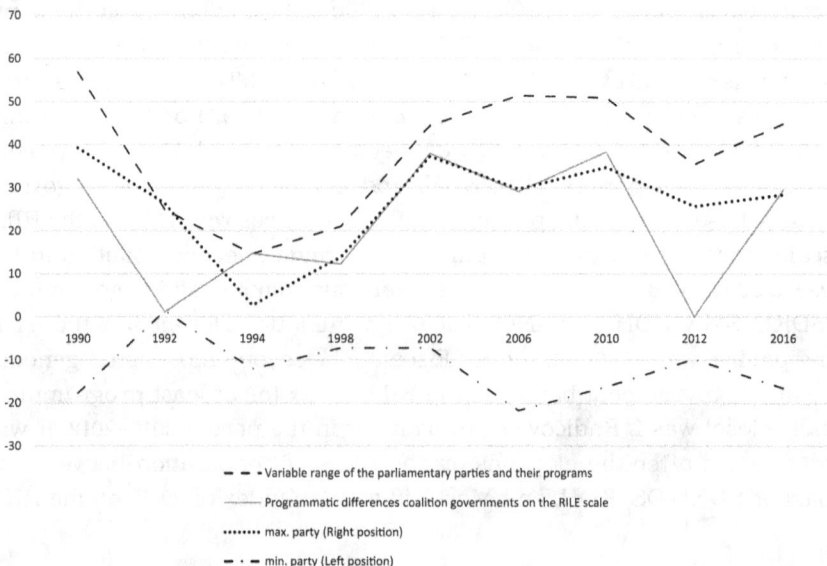

- – – Variable range of the parliamentary parties and their programs
- —— Programmatic differences coalition governments on the RILE scale
- ·········· max. party (Right position)
- – · – min. party (Left position)

The culmination of the programmatic differences of the parties in the Slovak party system in the observed period is noted in 2006 (RILE index of 51,44). After these elections, the variable tensions between the political parties slightly subsided, however, the original ideological polarization was maintained, which had a source in the atypical transformation cleavage mečiarism vs. antimečiarism from the 1990s. This development phase had a profound effect on the subsequent consolidation process of the democratic institutions and the cooperation between the political parties. Due to the style of the third Mečiar's government policies (1994–1998), this government met the requirements for an illiberal democracy with "incomplete competitive authoritarianism" (Kopeček, 2006: 197). Mečiar's government violated the principle of separation of powers, constitutional rights, it criminalized political opposition, disregarded the findings of the Constitutional Court, etc. – we can see the correlation between this development and the renewed cleavage concerning the form of the regime. This process included the prime minister's effort to concentrate power in the executive branch (horizontal deformation of democracy) and a rise in nationalism and illiberal style of politics, which was based on the search for the so-called inside and outside enemy among the political opponents of the government. These developments within the party system led to partisan polarization, which was multiplied by the exercise of ruling power by means of the zero-sum game strategies. In essence, these developments formed two blocs within the framework of the Slovak party system. A bloc of parties sheltered by the socio-nationalist rhetoric combined with an emphasis on Christian traditions. This was the case especially with HZDS and SNS (and ZRS in the period 1994–1998). The other half of the party spectrum represented the right-wing parties KDH, DS, and DÚ. These were joined by the social-democratic SDĽ after the political developments in 1994.[80] Due to the increased illiberal and nationalist tendencies of the ruling coalition in the years 1994–1998, the ethnic and regional parties of the Hungarian minority in Slovakia joined this bloc despite their leftist orientation after the integration into MK and later SMK. The fragmentation of the party system was not prevented even by the modification of the electoral law dur-

---

80 This fact, following the 1998 elections and the entry of SDĽ into Dzurinda's government, was one of the reasons for the departure of Robert Fico from SDĽ and establishment of a new left-wing party, which subsequently took over part of the SDĽ's electorate and caused its poor electoral results in 2002. The cooperation of SDĽ with the right-wing parties also had an impact on the transfer of some of its voters to KSS, which for the first time since 1990 made it into the Slovak Parliament. For more information on the volatility and structure of each of the popular voter bases in the years 1998 and 2002 see Kopeček, 2006: 233–236.

ing Mečiar's government in 1998. This created the conditions for greater cooperation and integration of the opposition parties, for example, SDK and SMK. On the other hand, the dissatisfaction with the style of politics of the incumbent party leaders led to the continual splitting and emergence of new parliamentary parties. In 1998, it was SOP, and in 2002 SMER, ANO and KSS. In 2010 it was SaS and Most-Híd and in 2012 OĽaNO.[81]

It is only in the period 2010–2012 that the programmatic differences between the parties on the extreme sides of the party system were observed to subside, and one could observe a programmatic convergence of the parliamentary parties because the variable range of the parliamentary parties in 2012 had a value of 35.39. However, due to the continuing fragmentation of the party system, the format of the party system did not change. It remained in the position of extreme multipartism. The lower degree of programmatic distance of the extremely leftist SMER-SD and extremely rightist SaS after the 2012 elections did not result in the reduction of ideological polarization of the party system. This continues to be absent, and in combination with the growing public skepticism toward the established parties, it created a potential for new parties making it into Parliament, as was the case in 2002. At that time, SMER assumed the position of a centrist right and released the space on the left of the political spectrum.

In the last parliamentary elections of 2016, the trend toward the fragmentation of the political spectrum was confirmed. New parties and movements, such as Network, We Are Family – Boris Kollár and the extremist party K-ĽS-NS, made it into the Parliament. The emergence of the latently antisystemic party K-ĽS-NS, which among other things wants the Slovak Republic to withdraw from the structures of the EU and NATO, and which is hallmarked by antisemitic and xenophobic manifestations, also caused polarization among the opposition parties. However, its emergence in the Parliament was not caused by emptying the extreme right part of the political spectrum as was the case with KSS on the left. At the same time, the existence of the extremist party K-ĽS-NS in the Parliament may be anything but short-lived because the polls and the results of the first round of presidential elections show (Marian Kotleba received 222,935 votes) that the euroscepticism-europeanism cleavage has stabilized in the Slovak party system. The potential for an increased relevance of extremist parties is also

---

81 Although the 2016 elections do not fall within the analyzed period, the 5% threshold was exceeded by the right-wing extremist party Kotleba People's Party Our Slovakia, the populist We Are Family – Boris Kollár (Sme Rodina- Boris Kollár) and the rightist-centrist Network (Sieť).

caused by the increasing distrust of the citizens in parliamentary parties and institutions of liberal democracy. Drawing on our hypothesis, which states that the convergence of political programs of the parties makes space for the establishment of extremist and/or antisystemic parties, we can conclude that this hypothesis was not confirmed until 2016. Since 1990, only two political parties that meet the attributes of an extremist or antisystemic party, made it into the Slovak Parliament. This happened in 2002 and 2016. In the last parliamentary elections of 2016, the increased public dissatisfaction with the established parties was also reflected in the election of the extremist party Kotleba ĽS-NS. The factors, such as mobilization of dissatisfied voters, protest votes and first-time voters, led to the entry of an extremist party into the Parliament. This party is the latently antisystemic right-wing extremist Kotleba-ĽS NS. Despite the fact that it shows no extreme values on the right side of the RILE scale in terms of its communication and the objectives of its leaders, we can conclude that it seeks to delegitimize the institutions of liberal democracy through its speeches (but not through the political program). In addition to meeting the attributes of a protest party, the right-wing extremist party K-ĽS-NS is the bearer of antisemitic, xenophobic, nationalist, and antiliberal values. The leading representatives of the party consider the Slovakia's accession to the EU structures to be a loss of national sovereignty and betrayal of national interests, and they advocate for a withdrawal from the EU and NATO. For this reason, Kotleba ĽS NS is not only a protest, antipolitical, and antiestablishment party, such as OĽaNO or We Are Family – Boris Kollár, but also a party, which ultimately stands in an ideological conflict with the liberal-democratic regime. For this reason, a proposal for dissolution has been filed even in the case of K-ĽS NS. The proposal was filed by Attorney General Jaromír Čižnár at the Supreme Court in May 2017. In April 2019, the Supreme Court began a hearing on the dissolution of K-ĽS NS. Due to its stable constituency and voter base (the polls for K-ĽS NS oscillate at around eight, -11.5%), even the potentially negative outcome of the dissolution trial may not mean an end of the parliamentary activities for the representatives of K-ĽS NS. In the event of their dissolution, the representatives of K-ĽS NS have registered a backup party People's Party Slovak Stronghold (Ľudová strana Pevnosť Slovensko). Martin Beluský, a friend and collaborator of M. Kotleba and currently an MP for K-ĽS NS, is its current chairman. The party K- ĽS NS was not dissolved by a decision of the Supreme Court of the Slovak Republic dated April 29, 2019. The reason was that the prosecutor did not provide sufficient evidence of antisystemic of Kotleba's party.

The emergence of an extremist party on the left side of the party system was noted in 2002. The entry of the extremely leftist KSS into the Parliament, however, did not mean its parliamentary establishment. At the same time, it should be noted that this was aided by the developments in SDĽ. Since 1994, when it was part of the Common Choice (RILE index of -12.06) election coalition, this party moved to the center in 1998 with a value of -6.25. This development has subsequently enabled the KSS to fill the left-wing space after SDĽ since the newly established SMER in that period represented a leftist-liberal, centrist-oriented alternative to the government coalition of M. Dzurinda. The British Labour Party led by Tony Blair was the model declared by SMER's leadership. The orientation of SMER after the failure in the 2002 elections (RILE index of a rightist-centrist party with a value of 8.86) has changed radically under the influence of smaller left-wing parties SDĽ, SOP, SDSS, SDA, and their integration into SMER. Before the parliamentary elections in 2006, the SMER's party leadership changed the focus of its agenda to highlight the social and nationalist themes, and it again filled the leftist spectrum with an index of -21.76. By changing the programmatic priorities and addressing the voters of KSS, SNS, and HZDS, SMER-SD secured its position as the strongest coalition party in the government. Despite its marxist-leninist aims and resistance against the integration of Slovakia into the Euro-Atlantic structures[82], the KSS under the leadership of Jozef Ševc split at the beginning of 2005 after the conflict between the regional structures.[83] After this split, the original KSS electorate scattered among the other minor leftist parties and non-voters. It should be noted that since the beginning of the transition period, Eastern Slovakia with its distinct socio-economic inequalities has always supported leftist formations, which criticized the consequences of the economic transformation from the 1990s. For this and other reasons, the voters from this region had a clear tendency to promote new parties with their protest vote. For example, in 1994 it was ZRS, in 1998 SOP, in 2002 KSS (Kopeček, 2007: 254–256)

---

82 KSS mentioned the entry of the Slovak Republic into the EU structures only in 2002. However, it conditioned it by Slovakia's economic preparedness. KSS remained ambivalent on this topic because it was the only parliamentary party that voted against the entry of the Slovak Republic into the EU due to the alleged disadvantages, but they advocated for joining the EU in the referendum.

83 A competing communist formation Úsvit under the leadership of Ivan Hopta was registered in 2005. The disintegration process of the KSS was caused by the dissatisfaction of the regional structures in Eastern Slovakia where the KSS had the highest support, with the leadership of the party. These regional structures challenged the chairman of the KSS Jozef Ševc and blamed him for low representation in the leadership of the party vis-a-vis the election results.

and in 2006 SMER-SD. It was only in this development stage of the party system (1998–2002) that the emptying of the leftist spectrum and efforts of most political parties to establish themselves in the center made a way for the parliamentary activity of KSS, which was a latently antisystemic party. However, it failed to establish itself in the party system in 2002–2006 and it remained an isolated parliamentary body. The position of the relevant left was then taken over by SMER-SD. This party completed the integration of smaller left-wing parties in 2004 and it attracted most of the left-wing voters. This made it a dominant body on the left.

At the same time, it was obvious that the victory of KSS in the 2002 parliamentary elections had no direct relation to the increase or decrease of variable tensions. Despite the fact that in 2002 the variable tensions between the parliamentary parties increased (from 21.04 in 1998 to 44.5 in 2002), the increase of variable tensions had no effect on the marginalization of KSS. The victory of KSS in the parliamentary elections was rather caused by emptying the leftist spectrum (most parties had rightist programs). To confirm this conclusion, we can use the development of programmatic orientation in the years 1992–1998. Even in this period, most parliamentary parties were centrist. However, a visible relaxation of the leftist spectrum was not observed. The variable tensions between the parliamentary parties in this period were at relatively low levels of 24.93 (1992), 14.72 (1994), and 21.04 (1998). Despite this fact, the reduction of programmatic differences of the parties in this period did not lead to the establishment of antipolitical, antiestablishment, antisystemic, or radical parties in the party system. Our hypothesis about the correlation between the decreasing programmatic differences of the parliamentary parties and the rise of extremist and antisystemic parties in the Slovak party system was not confirmed until 2012. This conclusion is also supported by the fact that, for example, even in 1992, the extreme left was represented by SDĽ with a RILE score of a centrist party (-1.41), a similar score was observed in 1998 with SMK (7.18), and despite this centrist orientation of the leftist parties, no extremist or antisystemic parties established themselves on the left.

Despite the fact that the hypothesis on the centrist orientation of the relevant political parties aiding the establishment of extremist parties in the Slovak party system was not confirmed up to 2012, the research into the development of the party system on the basis of the RILE index indicates that the image of some of the parties in light of their self-presentation and self-identification is not in harmony with their programmatic objectives. Let us mention DS as an example: in 1990, it presented itself as a conservative, right-wing civic entity, but its RILE index was the one of a leftist party

(RILE of -12.30). In 1992, SDĽ as a socialist or social democratic party had a RILE score of 1.41, that is, a centrist right score. In the election year 1994, the KDH had a score of -6.79, that is, with a predominance of leftist themes and solutions, and SNS as a nationalist, far right party had a program with a slight predominance of leftist topics at -1.54 on the RILE scale. The development of the party system and its ongoing ideological polarization in 2002 led the newly established SMER to publicly define itself as a liberal leftist party. However, rightist themes dominated in its program, with a RILE index of 8.86. In that year, even HZDS, which has long presented itself as a centrist body, moved significantly to the right with an index of 20.63. In 2006, after the two governments of M. Dzurinda and the economic reforms of his cabinet, the socio-economic cleavage became dominant in the party system. Even for this reason, the right-wing SDKÚ-DS as the bearer of fundamental economic changes in the years 1998–2006 moved to the position of a centrist party with a slight predominance of leftist themes and a RILE score of -1.25. This development trend in its program was subsequently confirmed in 2010 when the preponderance of leftist themes in the SDKÚ-DS program rose to -3.54 on the RILE scale. It tried to change its public image as a party that does not take account of the interests of low-income population groups.

It will be interesting to see how the parties develop programmatically in the future, and whether our hypothesis is confirmed when the new RILE index data for 2020 will be published. Other new parties made it into Parliament in the last parliamentary elections. They identified themselves on the right, and for the first time since 1990 they also included a right-wing extremist and ideologically antisystemic party K–ĽS NS. The new parties that have established themselves in Parliament since 2012 can be viewed as "protest" parties because they managed to mobilize the voters just to show their resistance to the established and incumbent parliamentary parties, that is, we can characterize them as antipolitical and antiestablishment (e.g., We Are Family – Boris Kollár, Kotleba – People's Party Our Slovakia, and OĽaNO since 2012).

Thus, the research of the party system after 2019 remains an open territory even in the WZB database because the developments indicate that the fragmentation of the party spectrum will continue in the future. The question of whether the development of the party system continues with the radicalization of political discourse and the long-term existence of an extremist party in the party system, which is indicated by the political developments in 2019, also needs to be answered. In the case of a long-term existence of an extreme right-wing party among the parliamentary parties

and the continued fragmentation of the party system, the political developments similar to those in Hungary after 2010 are not entirely excluded even
in Slovakia.

In the present publication, we have attempted to combine the empirical
and normative approach to the development of the party system in Slovakia and the characteristics of coalition governments. Given the broad ar-
ray of methodologies to examine the parties and party systems, we've once
again proved that regardless of the choice of a particular methodological
approach to examining the political processes (in our case, the RILE scale),
political parties, and party systems, the qualification approach introduced
by Giovanni Sartori in his work is key to understanding the development
tendencies in the party system. For example, the issue of antisystemicity
and possible extremist orientation of a political party cannot be determined solely on the basis of quantifying the selected aspects of its political
program. This was reflected in our research into, for example, K-ĽS NS or
KSS. None of the said parties exhibited their extremist ideological orientation on the RILE scale in a significant way. In the case of KSS in 2002, it
reached -7.14, which corresponds to the political program of a rather moderate centrist-leftist party rather than an ideologically extreme communist
formation. A similar situation was observed with K-ĽS NS when taking
into account its political program and present verbal expressions of its
leaders, which overtly or covertly show sympathy for antisemitism, racial,
and ethnic intolerance and the Slovak fascist state of 1939–1945. However,
in the case of K-ĽS NS, the RILE scale (a value of 8.99 from 2016) does not
visibly indicate its ideological antisystemicity in the liberal-democratic regime. When using comparative analysis as a research method to analyze
the party system and its development and the nature of coalition governments, our research showed the need for both approaches (qualification
and quantification) to understand the nature of political conflict, its practical implications for the lives of citizens, and taking into account the most
important cleavage lines in society.

In Hungary, the success of Jobbik changed the nature of political discourse and rhetoric, which turned radical particularly in the case of the
strongest right-wing party Fidesz. If K-ĽS NS can establish itself as an extremist party in the party system, we can also expect similar changes in
the nature of political discourse in Slovakia. The first such changes could
be noted in the 2016 elections where all parties assumed the anti-migration
rhetoric for the fear of loss of confidence on the part of the majority society.
After the elections, the parties agreed to isolate K-ĽS NS in the Parliament,
but experience has shown that some ruling parties did not hesitate to hold

negotiations with this party in the case of coalition disputes. The March 2019 example shows that the parliamentary groups of SMER and SNS with the support of K–ĽS NS and certain individuals from other parties can easily shake hands in an effort to constitutionally enshrine the law on the pension ceiling and/or retirement age. We can conclude that an increase in the voter support of K–ĽS NS and stabilization of its core voters may result in the transformation of their blackmailing potential into a covert coalition potential. This situation may also occur when K–ĽS NS receives enough mandates in the Parliament to block the formation of a functional government coalition. For this and other reasons, the consolidation of the party system in Slovakia can be characterized as unfinished because there is a general tendency for the emergence of new parties, which, however, do not contribute to the established structuralized party system, but fragment it even more in the presence of ideological and programmatic polarization. The emergence of new parties after the 2016 parliamentary elections is evidence of these trends. Progressive Slovakia (Progresívne Slovensko – PS) and Together – Civil Democracy (SPOLU) are the parties with the potential to become relevant actors also thanks to their pragmatic preelection coalition before the 2019 elections into the European Parliament. They won most votes (20.11%) in these elections, which determined the nature of their cooperation in the 2020 parliamentary elections. Such new parties also include the party "For the People" of the former president Andrej Kiska, which he founded with former co-workers and sympathizers from the Office of the President. All in all, there is a high probability of a further increase in the total amount of relevant parties with the blackmailing potential in the 2020 elections. The constant increase in the fragmentation of the parliamentary parties will probably be reflected in the growth of programming disparities of the parliamentary parties, which can further complicate the creation of stable and actionable coalition groups. In addition to the insufficiencies in the law on political parties, this situation is also caused by the electoral law to the Parliament. Despite the fact that it has the greatest impact on the creation of the party system and its functionality, this issue remains outside the area of concern for most of the parliamentary parties. When this normative problem is overlooked, it causes a decrease in the functionality and credibility of the parties in civic society. The risks of this development in the Slovak party system are reflected in the fragmentation of the party system and a visible increase in the support for anti-establishment or extremist, nationalist, and antisystemic parties, which the incumbent parties try to reduce by adjusting their programs, particularly in the socioeconomic area, and a parallel increase in the populist rhetoric aimed to satisfy the short-term interests of selected groups of population regardless of the long-term sustainability and social consequences. Since the changes in the electoral and political preferences are caused by several factors, such as decreasing citizen confidence in the political parties, parliament, and government, decline of political engagement of the democratically minded citizen groups[84] and activation of disaffected and apathetic citizens, political science needs to research and examine these development trends in the public preferences and formulate possible solutions to minimize their negative impact on democracy. This is one of the most important aims of the present publication: to build on the existing research in this area and complement it with new perspectives that can facilitate a comprehensive understanding of the relationship between the essential aspects determining the role of the electoral and party system in the development of political parties, political culture, and formation of civil liberal democratic society.

---

84 For more information on this issue, see Bútorová, Z.: Spoločenská klíma na Slovensku pred voľbami 2016 a po nich. In: Krivý, V. (ed.): Slovenské voľby 2016 retrospektívne analýzy. Bratislava: Sociologický ústav SAV, pp. 11–51.

Charts and Tables

Table Development of variable range of the parliamentary parties within the context of development of the coalition program differences on the RILE scale.

	Election 1990	Election 1992	Election 1994	Election 1998	Election 2002	Election 2006	Election 2010	Election 2012	Election 2016
Variable range of the parliamentary parties and their programs on the RILE scale	56,87	24,93	14,72	21,04	44,5	51,44	50,93	35,39	44,91
Programmatic differences of the coalition on the RILE scale	32,05 VPN, KDH, DS Minimum winning, program. homogen. coalition	1,06 HZDS, SNS 24,93 KDH, SDĽ, ADS, APR Minimum winning, program. homogen. coalition	14,72 HZDS, SNS, ZRS Minimum winning, program. homogen. coalition	12,33 SDK, SDĽ, SMK, SOP Constitutional program. homogen. coalition	37,96 SDKÚ, SMK, KDH, ANO Minimum winning program. homogen. coalition	29,11 SMER-SD, SNS, ĽS-HZDS Minimum winning, program. homogen. coalition	33,82 SDKÚ-DS, SaS, KDH, Most-Hid 38,27 + (OKS) Minimum winning, program. homogen. coalition	SMER-SD	29,48 SMER-SD, SNS, Most-Hid, Network Minimum win. and program. homogen. coalition
Turnout	95,39%	84,20%	75,65%	84,24%	70,06%	54,67%	58,83%	59,11%	59,82%

The following tables give us a clearer picture of the development of the parties and their right-to-left orientation, and they summarize the RILE values for each of the parties in the individual elections from 1990 to the elections in 2016.

Program heterogeneity according to the RILE index

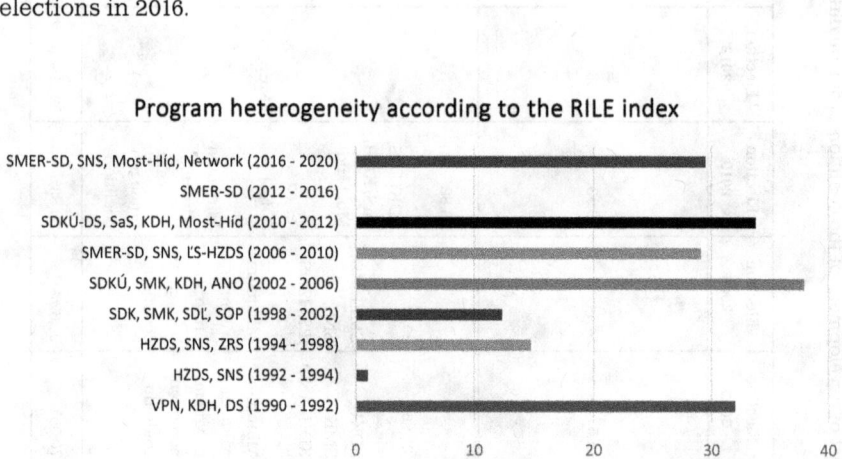

Source: Manifesto Project. Social Science Research Center Berlin [on line 25.4.2019] Available on https://visuals.manifesto-project.wzb.eu/mpdb-shiny/cmp_dashboard_dataset/

KDH - Christian Democratic Movement

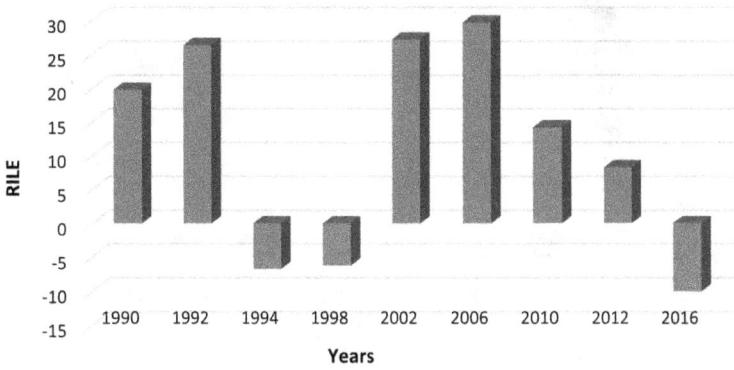

Development of the RILE index of KDH in the years 1990 - 2016

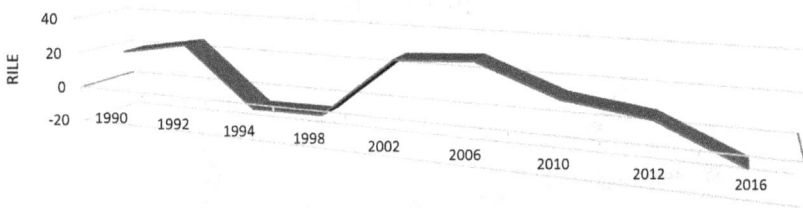

	1990	1992	1994	1998	2002	2006	2010	2012	2016
Development of the RILE index of KDH in the years 1990 - 2016	19,75	26,34	-6,79	-6,25	27,19	29,68	14,15	8,25	-10,07

SNS - Slovak National Party

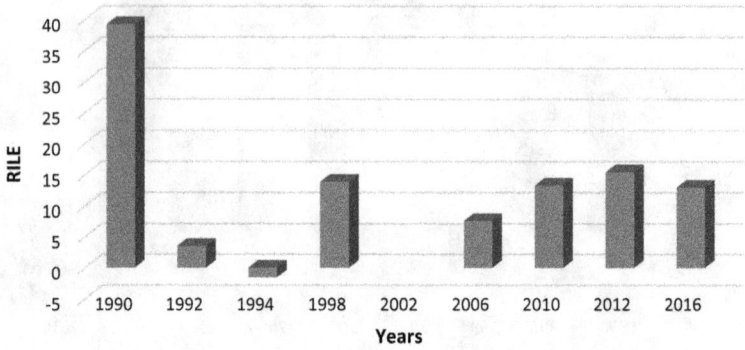

Development of the RILE index of SNS in the years 1990 - 2016

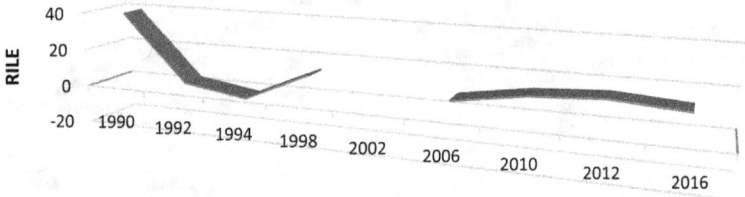

	1990	1992	1994	1998	2002	2006	2010	2012	2016
Development of the RILE index of SNS in the years 1990 - 2016	39,22	3,5	-1,54	13,86		7,59	13,28	15,42	12,95

ESWMK / MKM-EGY - Coalition of Coexistence and the Hungarian Christian
MK - Hungarian Coalition
SMK - Party of the Hungarian Coalition

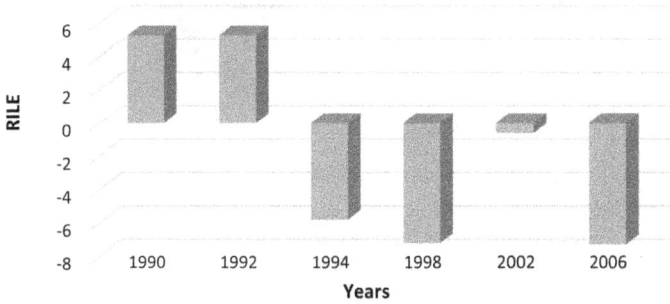

Development of the RILE index of ESWMK, MKM-EGY, MK, SMK in the years 1990 - 2006

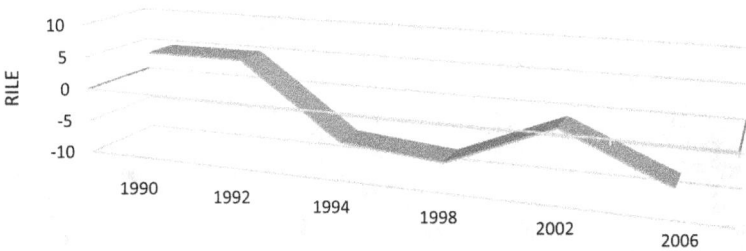

	1990	1992	1994	1998	2002	2006
Development of the RILE index of ESWMK, MKM-EGY, MK, SMK in the years 1990 - 2006	5,26	5,26	-5,79	-7,18	-0,6	-7,27

HZDS - Movement for a Democratic Slovakia
ĽS-HZDS - People Party - Movement for a Democratic Slovakia

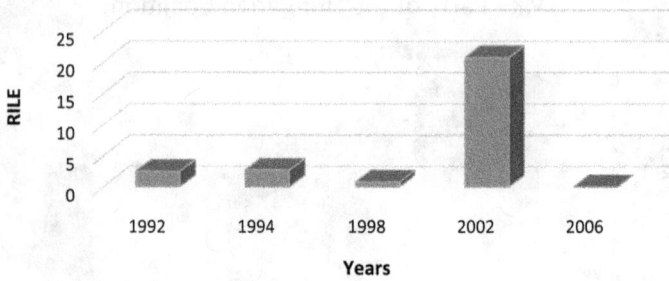

Development of the RILE index of HZDS, ĽS-HZDS in the years 1990 - 2006

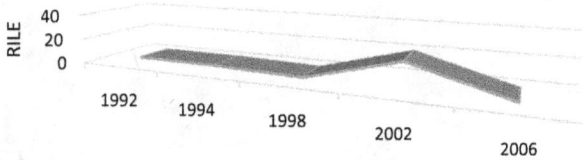

	1992	1994	1998	2002	2006
Development of the RILE index of HZDS, ĽS-HZDS in the years 1990 - 2006	2,44	2,66	0,75	20,63	0

SDĽ - Party of the Democratic Left
SV - Common Choice

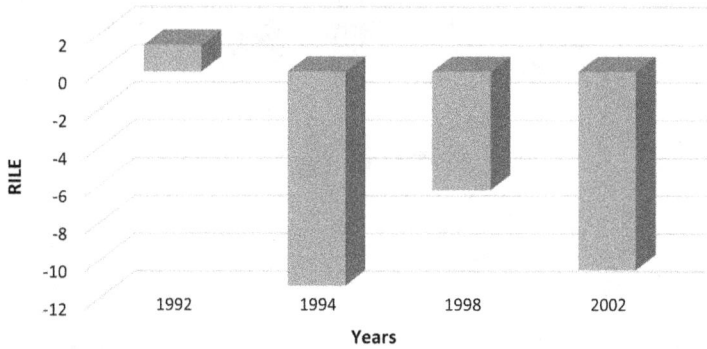

Development of the RILE index of SDĽ, SV in the years 1992 - 1998

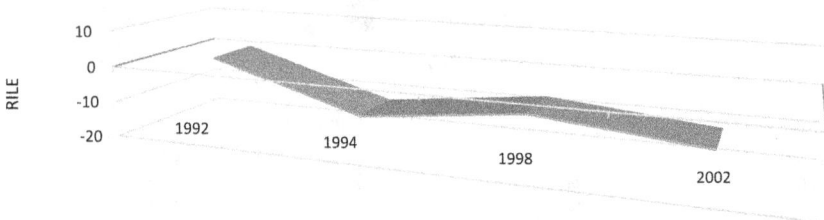

	1992	1994	1998	2002
Development of the RILE index of SDĽ, SV in the years 1992 - 1998	1,41	-11,32	-6,25	-10,49

SDK - Slovak Democratic Coalition
SDKÚ - Slovak Democratic and Christian Union SDKÚ-DS
- Slovak Democratic and Christian Union - Democratic
Party

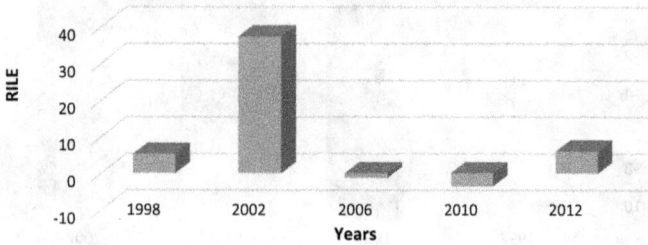

Development of the RILE index of SDK, SDKÚ, SDKÚ-DS in the
years 1998 - 2012

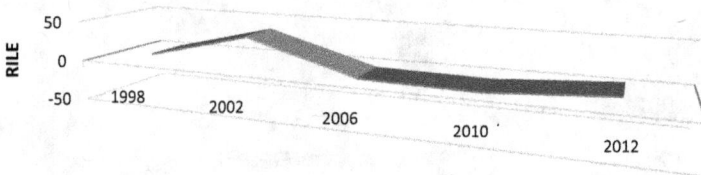

	1998	2002	2006	2010	2012
■ Development of the RILE index of SDK, SDKÚ, SDKÚ-DS in the years 1998 - 2012	5,19	37,28	-1,25	-3,54	6,03

SMER - Direction
SMER-SD - Direction - Social Democracy

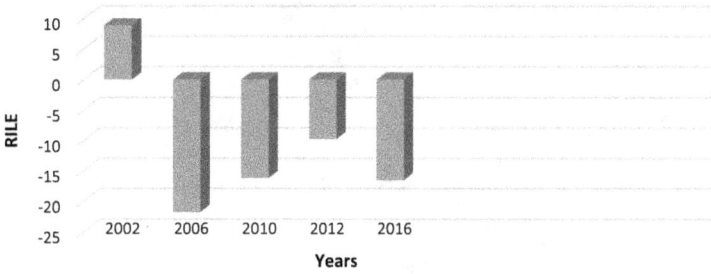

Development of the RILE index of SMER, SMER-SD years 1990 - 2016

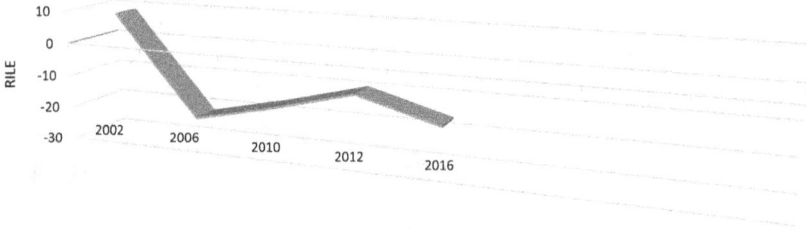

	2002	2006	2010	2012	2016			
Development of the RILE index of SMER, SMER-SD in the years 2002 - 2016	8,86	-21,76	-16,2	-9,73	-16,53			

Most-Híd - Bridge

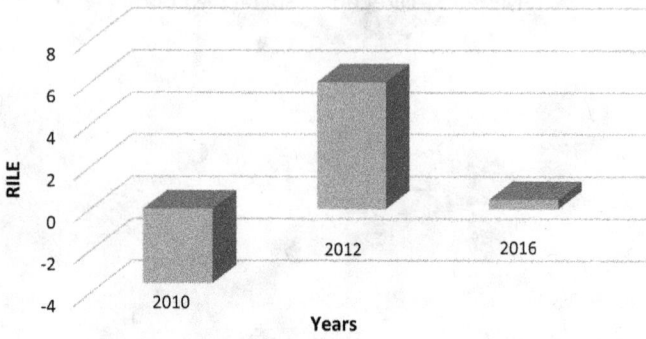

Development of the RILE index of Most-Híd in the years 2010 - 2016 - 2016

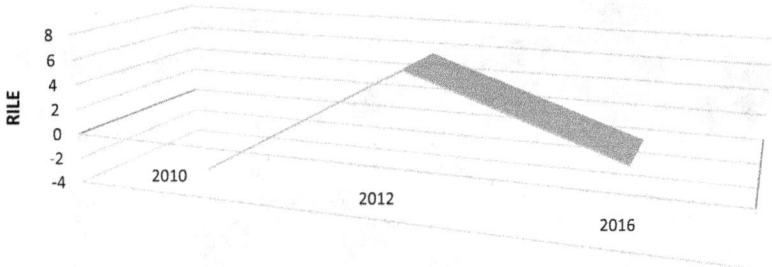

	2010	2012	2016
Development of the RILE index of Most-Híd in the years 2010 - 2016	-3,54	6,03	0,44

SaS - Freedom and Solidarity

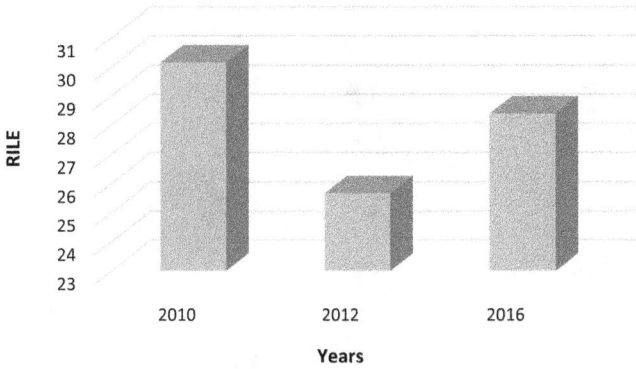

Development of the RILE index of SaS in the years 2010 - 2016

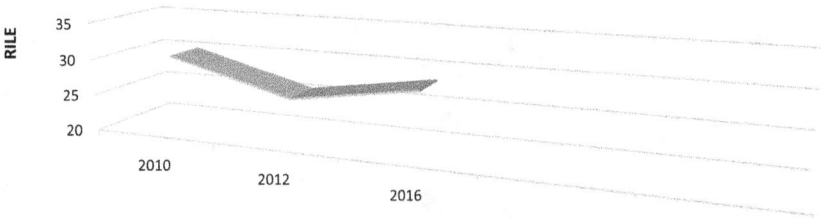

	2010	2012	2016		
Development of the RILE index of SaS in the years 2010 - 2016	30,15	25,66	28,38		

OĽaNO - Ordinary People and Independent Personalities

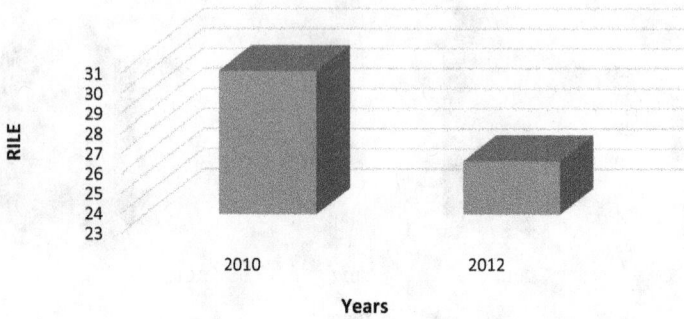

Development of the RILE index of OĽaNO in the years 2012 - 2016

	2010	2012
Development of the RILE index of OĽaNO in the years 2012 - 2016	30,15	25,66

Table Development of membership base of the parties in 2006–2017 (on December 31st of each year).

	2006	2010	2012	2014	2015	2016	2017
ĽS-HZDS	36064	28873	4175	–	–	–	–
KDH	17814 ↓	15360 ↓	13024 ↓	11704 ↓	11180 ↓	9807 ↓ In June 2016, Alojz Hlina replaced Ján Fígeľ as party chair	8948 ↑
SNS	1198	1839 ↑	2335 ↑ In October 2012 Andrej Danko replaced Ján Slota as party chairman	3884 ↑ In June 2016, Alojz Hlina replaced Ján Fígeľ as party chair	6155 ↑	7189 ↑	7662 ↑
SMER-SD	15132	16869 ↑	16 376 ↓	16167 ↓	15862 ↓	15605 ↓	15 182↓
SDKÚ-DS	8569	6842 ↓	4868 ↓ In May 2012 Pavol Frešo replaced Mikuláš Dzurinda as party chairman	6938 ↑	1179 ↓	396 ↓	–
SaS	–	271	292 ↑	166 ↓	154 ↓	164 ↑	208 ↑
SMK*, SMK-MKP	11959 2007 Pál Csáky replaced Béla Bugár as party chair	10750 ↓ 2010 József Berényi replaced P. Csáky as party chair	9800 ↓	10320 ↑	10075 ↓	9256 ↓ In June 2016 József Menyhárt replaced J. Berényi as party chair	9200 ↓
Most-Híd (Bridge)	–	4029	4892 ↑	5350 ↑	5414 ↑	5583 ↑	5517 ↓
KSS	8601	5207 ↓	5250 ↑	2136 ↓	2158 ↑	1769 ↓	1793 ↑
OĽaNO	–	–	4	4	4	13 ↑	13
ĽSNS, K-ĽS NS	?	11	162 ↑	45 ↓	96 ↑	796 ↑	1439 ↑
Network (Sieť)	–	–	–	966	1998 ↑	1560 ↓	–
We Are Family – Boris Kollár (Sme rodina – Boris Kollár)	–	–	–	–	5	450 ↑	1350 ↑

List of Abbreviations

ADS	Alliance of Democrats of the Slovak Republic
ANO	Alliance of the New Citizen
APR	Alternative to Political Realism
ARP	Protestant Anti-Revolutionary Party
CDA	Christian Democratic Appeal
CDU	Christian Democratic Union of Germany
CMP	Comparative Manifestos Project
CSU	Christian Social Union
CHU	Christian Historical Union
CU	Christian Union
DS-ODS	Democratic Party - Civic Democratic Party
DS	Democratic Party
DÚ	Democratic Union of Slovakia
D´66	Democrats 66
ESWMK/ MKM – EGY	Coalition of Coexistence and the Hungarian Christian-Democratic Movement
ESWS	Coexistence
FDP	Free Democratic Party
HZD	Movement for Democracy
HZDS	Movement for a Democratic Slovakia
KDH	Christian Democratic Movement
K–ĽS NS	Kotleba – People's Party Our Slovakia
KSČ	Communist Party of Czechoslovakia
KSS	Communist Party of Slovakia
KVP	Catholic People's Party
LPF	List Pim Fortuyn
ĽS	People's Party
ĽS NS	People's Party Our Slovakia
ĽS-HZDS	People Party – Movement for a Democratic Slovakia
MK	Hungarian Coalition
MKDH	Hungarian Christian Democratic Movement
MOS	Hungarian Civic Party
Most-Híd	Bridge
NATO	North Atlantic Treaty Organization
NaS-NS	Nation and Justice - Our Party

NEKA	Independent candidates
NR SR	National Council of the Slovak Republic
ODÚ	Civic Democratic Union
OKS	Civic Conservative Party
OĽ	Ordinary People
OĽaNO	Ordinary People and Independent Personalities
PES	Party of European Socialists
PS	Progressive Slovakia
PSNS	Original Slovak National Party
PVV	Party for Freedom
RILE	Right-left position
SaS	Freedom and Solidarity
SDA	Social Democratic Alternative
SDK	Slovak Democratic Coalition
SDKÚ	Slovak Democratic and Christian Union
SDKÚ-DS	Slovak Democratic and Christian Union – Democratic Party
SDĽ	Party of the Democratic Left
SDSS	Social Democratic Party of Slovakia
SF	Free Forum
Sieť	Network
SKDH	Slovak Christian Democratic Movement
SMER	Direction
SMER-SD	Direction – Social Democracy
SMK	Party of the Hungarian Coalition
SMK-MKP	Party of the Hungarian Community – Magyar Közösség Pártja
SNJ	Slovak National Unity
SNR	Slovak National Council
SMS	Party of Modern Slovakia
Sme rodina – Boris Kollár	We Are Family – Boris Kollár
SNS	Slovak National Party
SPD	Social Democratic Party of Germany
SP-NS	Slovak Congregation – National Party
SOP	Party of Civic Understanding
SPOLU	Together – Civil Democracy
SR	Slovak Republic
SV	Common Choice
SZS	Green Party of Slovakia
ÚS SR	Constitutional Court of the Slovak Republic
VPN	Public against Violence
VUC	Regional government

VVD	People's Party for Freedom and Democracy
V4	Visegrad Group
WZB	Wissenschaftszentrum Berlin für Sozialforschung
ZRS	Workers' Association of Slovakia

References

Balík, S., Havlík, V. et al. (2011): Koaliční vládnutí ve střední Evropě (1990 – 2010). Brno: IIPS, Masarykova univerzita.

Beyme, K. (1985): Political Parties in Western Democracies. Aldershot: Gower.

Buček, J., Plešivčák, M. (2017): Self-Government, Development and Political Extremism at the Regional Level: A Case Study from the Banská Bystrica Region in Slovakia. Sociológia, Vol. 49, No. 6, pp. 599–635. ISSN 0049 – 1225.

Budge, I., Meyer, T. (2013): Understanding and Validating the Left-Right Scale (RILE). In: Volkens, A. (ed.): Mapping Policy Preferences from Text: Statistical Solutions for Manifesto Analysts. New York: Oxford University Press, pp. 85–93.

Bútora, M., Ivantyšyn, M. et al. (1998): Slovensko 1997. Súhrnná správa o stave spoločnosti a trendoch na rok 1998. Bratislava: Inštitút pre verejné otázky.

Bútorová, Z. (2018): Spoločenská klíma na Slovensku pred voľbami 2016 a po nich. In: Krivý, V. (ed.): Slovenské voľby 2016 retrospektívne analýzy. Bratislava: Sociologický ústav SAV, pp. 11–51.

Duverger, M. (2016): Politické strany. Praha: Karolinum.

Gyárfášová, O. (2015): To sladké slovo demokracia ... Spokojnosť s demokraciou a politické odcudzenie na Slovensku. Sociológia, Vol. 47, No. 4, pp. 365–389. ISSN 0049 – 1225

Gyárfášová, O. (2018): Strany a voliči na ľavo-pravom kontinu: konvergencia alebo divergencia? In: Krivý, V. (ed.): Slovenské voľby 2016 retrospektívne analýzy. Bratislava: Sociologický ústav SAV, pp. 245–257.

Havlík, V., Kaniok, P. (ed.) (2006): Euroskepticizmus a země střední a východní Evropy. Brno: IIPS, Masarykova univerzita.

Katuninec, M. (2014): Režim slovenského štátu a jeho vývojové konotácie. In: Fiamová, M., Ilavinka, J., Schvarc, M. et al. (ed.): Slovenský štát 1939 – 1945: prodstavy a realita. Bratislava: Historický ústav SAV, pp. 125–136.

Keller, J. (2001): Politika s ručením omezeným: proměny moci na prahu 21. století. Praha: Evropský literární klub.

Klicperová-Baker, M., Feierabend, I. et al. (2007): Demokratická kultura v České republice. Praha: Academia.

Klíma, M. (2001): Kvalita demokracie v České republice. Praha: Radix.

Klíma, M. (2015): Od totality k defektní demokracii. Praha: Slon.

Kopeček, L. (2006): Demokracie, diktatury a politické stranictví na Slovensku. Brno: Centrum pro studium demokracie a kultury.

Kopeček, L. (2007): Politické strany na Slovensku 1989 až 2006. Brno: Centrum pro studium demokracie a kultury.

Kubát, M. (2010): Politická opozice v teorii a středoevropské praxi. Praha: Dokořán.

Kupka, P., Laryš, M., Smolík, J. (2009): Krajní pravice ve vybraných zemích střední a východní Evropy. Brno: IIPS, Masarykova univerzita.

Leška, D. (2013): Politický systém Slovenskej republiky. Bratislava: Univerzita Komenského.

Madleňák, T. (2012): Regionálna diferenciácia volebného správania na Slovensku (1998-2010). Bratislava: VEDA.

Marchuk V. (2016): Church, Spirituality, Nation. Ivano-Frankivsk: Play, 2016.

Marchuk V. (2008): The Political System of Ukraine: Problems of Formation and Development. Ivano-Frankivsk: Publishing and Design Department of CIT.

Novák, M. (ed.) (2016): Strany, volby a demokracie. Praha: Slon.

Pinterič, U., Žúborová, V. (2014): Party Areas in Slovenia and Slovakia. Vol. 23, No. 2, pp. 349-368. [on line 5.5.2019] Available on: http://drustvena-istrazivanja.pilar.hr/index.php/drustvena-istrazivanja/issue/view/30.

Sartori, G. (1993): Teória demokracie. Bratislava: Archa.

Sartori, G. (2001): Srovnávací ústavní inženírství. Praha: Slon.

Sartori, G. (2005): Strany a stranícke systémy. Brno: Centrum pro studium demokracie a kultury.

Schedler, A. (2002): Elections Without Democracy. The Menu of Manipulation. Journal of Democracy, Johns Hopkins University Press, Vol. 13. No. 2, pp. 36-50. ISSN 1045-5736.

Šedo, J. (ed.) (2003): Evropská otázka ve volebních kampaních. Brno: IIPS, Masarykova univerzita.

Wojtas, K. (2017): Coalition Politics in Poland in the Years 1991-2015 - in search of rules. In: Rudowski, A., Sulkowski, M. et al. (ed.): Poland in the European Union - perspectives of membership. Warsaw: CSWUP, pp. 23-45.

Internet

Bútorová, Z., Gyárfášová, O., Slosiarik, M. (2012). Public opinion and voting behavior. [on line 25.4.2019] Available on https://alianciazien.files.wordpress.com/2014/10/volby-2012-od-zb.pdf.

Bútorová, Z., Mesežnikov, G. et al. Aktívne občianstvo a občianska participácia na Slovensku a v krajinách V4. [on line 10.3.2019] Available on http://www.ivo.sk/buxus/docs//rozne/Prezentacia_IVO_19_12_Aktivne_obcianstvo.pdf.

Gyárfášová, O., Slosiarik, M. (2016): Voľby do NR SR 2016: Čo charakterizovalo voličov. Working Papers in Sociology 1. [on line 5.5.2019] Available on http://www.sociologia.sav.sk/pdf/Working_Papers_in_Sociology_012016.pdf.

Gyárfášová, O., Bahna, M., Slosiarik, M. (2017): Sila nestálosti: volatilita voličov na Slovensku vo voľbách 2016. Středoevropské politické studie, Vol. 19, No. 1, pp. 1-24. ISSN 1212-7817. [on line 5.5.2019] Available on: https://journals.muni.cz/cepsr/article/view/6861.

Haughton, T., Malova, D., Deegan-Krause, K. (2016): „Slovakia's newly elected parliament is dramatically different and pretty much the same. Here's how," The Washington Post, 9. 3. [on line 5.5.2019] Available on: https://www.washingtonpost.com/news/monkey-cage/wp/2016/03/09/slovakias-newly-elected-parliament-is-dramatically-different-and-pretty-much-the-same-heres-how/).

Haydanka, Y. I. (2018): Political and party environment fragmentation at a regional level in the light of local elections in the Czech Republic. In: Tomsk State University Journal of Philosophy, Sociology and Political Science. 45. pp. 184–193. [on line 5.5.2019] Available on: http://journals.tsu.ru/philosophy/en/&journal_page=archive&id=1770&article_id=39679.

Haydanka, Y. I. (2020): Urgent Decentralization Problems In The Czech Republic At A Regional Level: Political, Administrative And Sociological Dimensions. In: Public Policy and Administration. 2020, Vol. 19, No 2, pp. 253–265. DOI: 10.13165/VPA-20-19-2-08 [on line 15.7.2020] Available on: https://www3.mruni.eu/ojs/public-policy-and-administration/

Klus, M., Martinkovič, M., (2019): The Fragmentation of political representation at municipal level in Slovak republic in period 2002-2018. In: AD ALTA: Journal of Interdisciplinary Research. Vol. 9, No 2, pp. 193–198. DOI: 10.33543/2.0908193198 [on line 15.7.2020] Available on: http://www.magnanimitas.cz/ADALTA/0902/papers/A_martinkovic.pdf

Martinkovič, M. (2018): Phenomenon of independent candidates in the regional elections in Slovakia from 2001 to 2017. In: Politicus. No 2, pp. 55-60. DOI: 10.241945/2414-9616-2018-2-55-60 [on line 15.7.2020] Available on: http://politicus.od.ua/2_2018/11.pdf

Statistical office of the Slovak Republic. [on line 26.4.2019] Available on http://volby.statistics.sk/index.html.

Statistical Office of the Slovak Republic. [on line 25.4.2019] Available on http://volby.statistics.sk/nrsr/snr1990/volby90_s/pph90.htm.

Statistical Office of the Slovak Republic. [on line 26.4.2019] Available on http://volby.statistics.sk/nrsr/snr1992/volby92s/pph92.htm.

Statistical Office of the Slovak Republic. [on line 25.4.2019] Available on http://volby.statistics.sk/nrsr/nrsr1994/slov/volby22.htm.

Statistical Office of the Slovak Republic. [on line 25.4.2019] Available on http://volby.statistics.sk/nrsr/nrsr1998/results/tab2.jsp.htm.

Statistical Office of the Slovak Republic. [on line 25.4.2019] Available on http://volby.statistics.sk/nrsr/nrsr2002/webdata/vysledky_a.htm.

Statistical Office of the Slovak Republic. [on line 25.4.2019] Available on http://volby.statistics.sk/nrsr/nrsr2010/menu/indexv.jsp@lang=en.htm.

Wissenschaftszentrum Berlin für Sozialforschung (WZB), Social Science Research Centre Berlin - provides the data within the Comparative Manifestos Project (CMP) [on line 26.4.2019] Available on https://visuals.manifesto-project.wzb.eu/mpdb-shiny/cmp_dashboard_dataset/.

Register

Summary

This publication focuses on the characterization of the Slovak party system and its analysis from the perspective of cleavages and emerging government groups. The monograph also includes a description of the individual types of emerging government coalitions and their politological analysis on the basis of the RILE index (Right-left positioning). The said index is used to specify the programmatic differences of the emerging coalition governments and the impact of the development of the party system in Slovakia on their nature in the period from 1990 to 2012. The work is focused on the development trends of the Slovak party system on the background of programmatic homogeneity/heterogeneity of the individual coalition groups and the overall development of the variable tensions in the party system. The categorization of the government groups is based on the positional and programmatic orientation of the parties, which was published in the framework of the international database CMP (Comparative Manifestos Project). The Wissenschaftszentrum Berlin für Sozialforschung (WZB) database processes, inter alia, the data relating to the political programs of the parties within the framework of their comprehensive ideological orientation. The Center for Social Research in Berlin thus contains relevant internationally acceptable comparisons of the party systems and their development. The aim of this publication is to characterize the format and type of the party system in Slovakia, its consolidation and the resulting operational problems between the election system and party system.

The aim is also to extend the analysis of the Slovak party system to the specification of positional values and programmatic orientation of the parties in Slovakia based on the internationally accepted database and the RILE criteria. The publication also contains the tables with data on the proximity of variable tensions in the party system after each parliamentary elections and the relevant quantification on the RILE scale. The RILE scale will help us assess the programmatic homogeneity of the government coalitions also in view of the political discourse on this issue. The work will also verify the hypothesis that the programmatic convergence of the parties in the left-right spectrum creates space for the emergence and establishment of extremist and antisystemic parties in the parliamentary establishment.

About Author

Marcel Martinkovič is science-teaching staff in the Department of Political Science Faculty of Arts, University of Trnava. He specializes in the subject of History of Political Thought, comparing political systems, electoral and party systems, particularly in the context of transformation and democratization processes, problems of nationalism, ideas of Slavs and selected aspects of the crisis of democracy. On the parallel, he is dedicated to the research and development issues of Slovak political thinking in especially in the 19th century, in cooperation with the Institute of Philosophy of Slovak Academy of Sciences. Within the research of formation and development of Slovak national ideology, he is the author of the monograph The Political Thought of the New School, 2013 (Politické myslenie Novej školy); and editor and co-author of the collective monograph Ideas and Development of the Slovak Nation-Thinking in the 19th Century, 2011 (Idey a vývoj slovenského národotvorného myslenia v 19. storočí).

www.ingramcontent.com/pod-product-compliance
Lightning Source LLC
Chambersburg PA
CBHW050536270326
41926CB00015B/3254